WITHIN WHICH VEIL?

A RESPONSE TO J. ISAAC RICHARDS'
WITHIN THE VEIL AND SUBSEQUENT
MATERIAL QUESTIONING THE BIBLICAL
VIEWS OF THE HEAVENLY SANCTUARY,
INVESTIGATIVE JUDGMENT,
AND ATONEMENT

BY

JAMAL J. SANKEY

TEACH Services, Inc.
P U B L I S H I N G
www.TEACHServices.com • (800) 367-1844

Copyright © 2024 Jamal J. Sankey
Copyright © 2024 TEACH Services, Inc.
ISBN-13: 978-1-4796-1766-1 (Paperback)
ISBN-13: 978-1-4796-1767-8 (ePub)
Library of Congress Control Number: 2024906069

Published by

TEACH Services, Inc.
P U B L I S H I N G
www.TEACHServices.com • (800) 367-1844

TABLE OF CONTENTS

FOREWORD

In this excellent apologetic work, the author dismantles the standard arguments against the heavenly sanctuary doctrine taught by Seventh-day Adventists. These contentions are usually raised by those who previously held these theological tenets as present truth but now have abandoned their former position and joined the ranks of the opposition. *Within Which Veil?* demonstrates that these notions—a heavenly sanctuary without a second veil dividing two apartments, a stationary throne in the most holy place, a finished atonement at the cross, once saved always saved, no judgment for the saints, the sins of the little horn pollute the sanctuary, blood cleanses but does not defile, all faithful Christians constitute the remnant church of Bible prophecy—are not in harmony with sound biblical principles of prophetic interpretation. When the word of truth is rightly divided, the law and the testimony sustain this central pillar of the Adventist faith. The sanctuary truth stands as a firm platform in truth and righteousness as it has since the light was first given after the great disappointment of the second advent movement.

This book proves that the objections brought against the heavenly sanctuary, the atonement, the investigative judgment, and the cleansing of the sanctuary in Daniel 8 are a fulfillment of the apostle Peter's words, "They that are unlearned and unstable wrest ... scriptures, unto their own destruction" (2 Peter 3:16). Several times, the author takes J. Isaac Richards's arguments and turns them against his private interpretations. Theories that seem to destroy or undermine the Seventh-day Adventist movement's theological heartbeat are exposed as contradictions, built upon the sand of surface reading when tested by the Scriptures. Instead of proving that Seventh-day Adventist teachings regarding the great disappointment of 1844 are a fluke of prophecy, the scriptural analysis of *Within Which Veil?* compels us to conclude that we have "a more sure word of prophecy" and that "we have not followed cunningly devised fables" (2 Peter 1:19, 16). The type in the earthly sanctuary and the antitype in the heavenly sanctuary do not contradict each other, for their "builder and maker is God" who is the same "yesterday, to day, and for ever" (Heb. 11:10, 13:8).

We are admonished through the testimony of Jesus Christ that the people of God should clearly understand the subject of the sanctuary and the investigative judgment. All need knowledge of the position and work of their great High Priest. Otherwise, it will be impossible for them to exercise the faith that is essential at this time or to occupy the position that God designed them to fill. We are also warned about every kind of deception arising in these last days, wherein the enemy will bring in false theories; one of these is the doctrine that there is no sanctuary. That is one of the points on which there will be a departing from the faith by those who are "giving heed to seducing spirits, and doctrines of devils" (1 Tim. 4:1).

If you want solid ground for your feet and solid pillars for the building of your most holy faith so that you may be settled into the truth both intellectually and spiritually, so that you cannot be moved from the hope of the everlasting gospel, then I highly recommend this book, *Within Which Veil?* After studying this material, you will be able to affirm your faith in the sanctuary message, which is a complete system of truth, and also to defend the faith that was once delivered to the saints against false teachers and defectors. May the Holy Spirit guide each student of prophecy to drink from the living fountains of sound doctrine contained in this book and to refuse to drink from the broken cisterns of falsehood and confusion that can hold no water.

Elder Darrio D. Taylor
Senior Pastor, The Three Angels Fellowship
Speaker, Sure Word Ministry

INTRODUCTION

The public circulation of the document titled *Within the Veil* by J. Isaac Richards, as well as his subsequent material, regrettably necessitates an open response. There has been no small stir created by it, and whether that was the author's intention is not the purpose or scope of this reply. Notwithstanding, he intends to trumpet his public exit from Seventh-day Adventism into the Baptist communion and burden others with his almost constant barrage of emails, videos, and papers. While falling away is not a new experience in the history of the Christian church, it certainly hits close to home when it happens to people alongside which one has labored in the trenches of public ministry.

While intending to manifest Christian courtesy when addressing the points raised by Richards, we are authorized to call sin by its right name and believe that doing so is consistent with true charity. We will point out the errors and inconsistencies in his material so he and those who sympathize with his views should not have the slightest presumptuous encouragement. We believe God requires His people to stand unflinchingly for the right in opposition to soul-destroying errors.

Even though we strongly disagree with the sentiments embodied in his treatise, we genuinely love brother Richards. We pray that, after stepping off the platform of truth to examine it and declare it wrong, through our thorough search of the Scriptures to recount the wonderful work of God, which has led us to stand firmly upon the platform, he and those led astray by his notions will be affected, humbled, and prompted to step upon it again.

After proclaiming his loss of faith in the prophetic ministry of Ellen White and the doctrine of the investigative judgment, Richards proposes ten arguments in *Within the Veil*, which, in his mind, offer a biblical basis for his doubts. While the bulk of this response addresses that paper, some points address other material, such as that promoted on his website, which he has seen fit to publicize in its wake. We direct the reader to his publicized content for comparison. His points—cited in full in block quotes at the beginning of each chapter—and our subsequent replies will follow this brief introduction.

Also, note that there are numerous spelling, punctuation, and grammar mistakes in Richards' document left unchanged to indicate meticulous accuracy in reproducing his text; this goes for the other references used throughout this paper, though to a lesser degree.

We propose to furnish the reader with original lines of reasoning, though much of what Richards has addressed is a rehashing of errors raised by A. F. Ballenger, Desmond Ford, and others. Therefore, we will cite the works of those who addressed similar errors in the past, allowing the dead to speak. In the end, we are confident that the reader will have a better understanding of and biblical defense for the doctrines of the atonement, investigative judgment, and Christ's high priestly ministry in the heavenly sanctuary.

The Bible is clear that God's presence and throne were symbolized by the Shekina [sic] glory which appeared over the mercy seat of the ark which was only kept in the most holy place and not the holy. See Ex. 25:22; 30:5; Lev. 16:2; Numbers 7:89; 1 Samuel 4:4; 1 Kings 8:6; 1 Chronicles 13:6; Isaiah 37:16; Psalm 99:1; Hebrews 9:5. God's throne was never placed in the holy place. Neither is the table of showbread ever described anywhere in the Bible as an alternate throne. The throne of God had to be the ark since it's [sic] foundation was the law. Psalm 97:2; Isaiah 33:22. Therefore, to place the throne of God in the holy place of the heavenly sanctuary instead of the most holy place destroys the type and contradicts the scriptures. The earthly was built as a pattern of the heavenly and cannot contradict it. See Hebrews 8:5.[1]

The principle of type and antitype here is an important one that carries eternal implications. When Moses was instructed by the Lord to "speak ye unto the rock before their eyes; and it shall give forth his water" (Num. 20:8), that rock was a type of Christ (see 1 Cor. 10:1–4). Moses' disobedience in striking the rock twice tarnished the figure the Lord sought to teach. As a result, He barred Moses from entering the land of Canaan, promised to the children of God (see Num. 20:12). Though unintentional, Moses changed the type designed to teach us that after the

---

1   J. Isaac Richards, Within the Veil (Gakona, AK: Independent Seventh Day Bible Baptist Association, 2019), p. 2. https://www.isdba.org/_files/ugd/bcdc7f_8eafd31002ea4e7ab103ae6393cf1ba7.pdf.

Rock was smitten once on our behalf, all that is necessary is for us to speak to Him for the refreshing water of life to flow freely. Our Savior was "once offered to bear the sins of many" (Heb. 9:28), yet Moses' lack of restraint marred that figure.

To change, find fault in, or deny a type affects the truth associated with it—this is the idea raised in the first point under consideration. A type is an example, shadow, or figure of an antitype (see Exod. 25:8, 9, 40; 1 Chron. 28:11–19; Heb. 8:5; 9:1–9, 23, 24). Understanding this point will serve as a solid foundation for our rebuttal. It will show that *Within the Veil* repudiates the principle of type and antitype by the arguments raised therein, though often mentioned throughout.

Along with the principle of type and antitype addressed in the paper, other ideas are put forth in his first point: namely, that "God's throne was never placed in the holy place" and that "the table of showbread" is never "described anywhere in the Bible" as the throne of God.[2] A simple Bible study will reveal that the heavenly prototype set the pattern for every article of furniture in the earthly sanctuary copy (see Exod. 25:8–40) and the Lord has revealed said prototypes in the heavenly to confirm their earthly type.

John, while in the Spirit, saw "a door ... opened in heaven" and "seven lamps of fire burning ... which are the seven Spirits of God" (Rev. 4:1, 5). These "seven lamps" are the antitype of the menorah placed on the southern side of the earthly sanctuary's holy place (see Exod. 40:24), though John saw into the heavenly. He was again permitted to see the ministry of an angel who "came and stood at the altar, having a golden censer; and there was given unto him much incense, that he should offer it with the prayers of all saints upon the golden altar which was before the throne" (Rev. 8:3). A careful reading of the Scriptures shows that there was no other entrance opened before John between chapters 4 and 8 and he, as well as those who read, are still in the holy place of the heavenly temple. Therefore, this "golden altar"

2   *Ibid.*

finds its type in the altar of incense in the earthly holy place (see Exod. 30:1–6; 40:26) positioned towards the west of the sanctuary "before the vail." The typical service performed at this altar on the Day of Atonement provides further evidence that its location was outside the veil (see Lev. 16:12, 13).

The Lord employs further proof that John saw into the holy place of the heavenly temple by mentioning the "four and twenty elders" (Rev. 4:4) who are the counterpart of the twenty-four courses of priests (see 1 Chron. 24:1–19; 2 Chron. 8:14). Jesus, introduced to the reader of the Apocalypse as the high priest by His attire (see Rev. 1:12, 13), brings the number of priests to twenty-five, further fulfilling the type: twenty-four chief priests and one high priest (see Ezek. 8:16). It is important to note that only the high priest was able to enter the Most Holy Place of the sanctuary (see Heb. 9:6, 7; cf. Lev. 16:2–20). Therefore, when the prophet saw the vision of the "four and twenty seats: and upon the seats I saw four and twenty elders sitting, clothed in white raiment" (Rev. 4:4), this was no doubt the Holy Place since the high priest alone has access to the Most Holy.

These "four and twenty elders" are again seen in Revelation 11 just before "the temple of God was opened in heaven" for the second time (verse 19). Remember, their location in the type denotes the Holy Place, so seeing them again before the temple opens marks the opening of the door into the Holiest of all, where we see "the ark of his testament." The type met its antitype in the seven-branched candlestick, altar of incense, ark of the testament, and order of the priesthood. However, what about the table of showbread? If all that was shown Moses (see Exod. 25:8, 9, 40) and David (see 1 Chron. 28:11–19) were patterns of the heavenly; indeed, the antitype of this table should be found in heaven. If we turn to the first time John saw a view into the heavenly temple, we can find only one thing that would correlate to the table of showbread: the throne (see Rev. 4:1–5).

Richards argues that "the table of showbread" is never "described anywhere in the Bible as an alternate throne."[3] If the throne mentioned in Revelation 4 is not the antitype of the table of showbread, what is and where is it found? Would the Lord verify the other aspects of the type and leave out such a crucial piece as the table containing the bread of the presence (see Exod. 25:30)?[4]

---

3   *Ibid.*

4   The Hebrew for "shewbread" is *pânîym* or *pâneh*, meaning "face(s), presence, in front of, before, to the front of, in the presence of, in the face of, at the face or front of, from the presence of, from before, from before the face of" (see *Brown-Driver-Briggs' Hebrew Definitions*, H6440). Therefore, the word "shewbread" literally means "bread of faces" or "bread of the presence" because it was placed before the presence or face of God in the sanctuary.

The northern side of the holy place contained the table of showbread (see 26:35; 40:22); it was the location of the throne of God coveted by Lucifer (see Isa. 14:13; cf. Ps. 48:1, 2). This illustrious table's construction contained crowns (see Exod. 25:23–27; 37:12), and a crown denotes a ruler or king (see 2 Kings 11:12; Ps. 21:1–3). One of the symbols represented by the bread on the table is the Word of God (see John 6:32–34, 53–63), and the word comes from the north (see Dan. 11:44; cf. Amos 8:12). The throne, the king's crown, and the Word of God, all on the sides of the north, are beautiful symbols the table and showbread illustrate. Furthermore, the bread in the north situated on the throne alludes to the true King of the North, but space does not permit following that train of thought here in this response. Thus, the table of showbread, typifying God's throne in the heavenly sanctuary's Holy Place, rather than destroying the type and contradicting the Scriptures, shows the excellent continuity between the earthly and heavenly temples.

Richards reasons, "God's presence and throne were symbolized by the Shekina [sic] glory which appeared over the mercy seat of the ark which was only kept in the most holy place and not the holy."[5] That argument attempts to keep God fixed in the Most Holy Place, yet the Bible often shows Him in the Holy Place (see Exod. 29:38–46; 33:8–11; 2 Chron. 5:13, 14). Furthermore, the Bible illustrates an essential point about a king's throne: that it is movable (see 2 Chron. 18:9; Esther 1:2; 5:1), even showing God's throne as being fashioned with wheels to denote its mobility (see Dan. 7:9, 10; Ezek. 1:4–28; 10:1–22). A great Bible student explained it this way:

> The Bible was written in an oriental country, and the custom there is to "cast down seats for guests." The Revised Version of the Bible renders it, "I beheld till the thrones were placed." The position of the Father's throne was changed. Daniel beheld the thrones cast down, or placed, their position being changed; then the Ancient of days, the Father, took His seat upon the throne. In other words, Daniel beheld the Father's throne changed from the first apartment of the heavenly sanctuary to the second. His attention was attracted by the great wheels which looked like burning fire as they moved beneath the glorious throne of the infinite God (Ezek. 10:1–22). Myriads of the heavenly host were gathered to witness

5   Within the Veil, p. 2.

the grand scene. Thousand thousands ministered unto Jehovah as He took His seat upon the throne to judge the world ...

God's throne is a movable structure. As in the type His visible presence was manifested in the outer apartment of the earthly sanctuary, so in heaven the throne of God was in the first apartment when Christ ascended and sat at the right hand of His Father. But Daniel saw not only the Father and Christ change their position, but the position of the thrones also was changed, when the "judgment was set, and the books were opened." Type had met antitype. The High Priest in the heavenly sanctuary entered the most holy place, and as in the type God promised to meet the high priest in the most holy, so the Father passed into the holy of holies before the High Priest, and was there when the angels bore Christ triumphantly in before Him.[6]

For those who have eyes to see, a beautiful picture emerges. We see that the glorious presence of God and His throne were never inherently fixed in the Holiest of holies but moved as the plan of salvation required. Richards said, "The earthly was built as a pattern of the heavenly and cannot contradict it."[7] Yes, dear brother, we strongly agree.

---

6   Stephen N. Haskell, The Cross and Its Shadow (South Lancaster, MA: The Bible Training School, 1914), pp. 212–214.

7   Within the Veil, p. 2.

First, the fact that there is a sanctuary in heaven is abundantly plain in scripture. Psalm 11:4; Revelation 11:19; 15:5; 16:7; Hebrews 8:1. Some will refer to Revelation 4:5 in an attempt to prove that God's throne was at one time in the holy place since it is stated that the seven lamps of fire (a reference to the seven branched golden candlestick of the earthy tabernacle that was in the holy place) was "before the throne". However, a careful reading of the scripture does not allow the throne of God to be in the holy place. This claim is based on trying to show that, from the type, the candlestick was directly facing the table of showbread; therefore, it is reasoned, that the throne must be the table of showbread. However, the altar of incense is also said to be "before the throne" (See Revelation 8:3); yet it is obvious that the incense altar was placed directly before the veil which faced the ark of the covenant which symbolized the throne of God, and not the table of showbread. Further, the Bible itself is clear that both the candlestick and incense altar were placed before the ark in the Old Testament type. See Ex. 30:1–6; Lev. 24:1–4; Ex. 40:24, 25; 1 Kings 7:49; 2 Chronicles 4:20. Based on those aforementioned scriptures, in order to harmonize the testimony of scripture, and to allow the Bible to explain itself, John the revelator simply saw what the type proves: that is, the throne of God in the most holy place, before which were placed the incense altar and candlestick. The reason why this could be is based simply on the fact that there is no literal veil in heaven separating the holy and most holy places. "All is terror and

confusion. *The priest is about to plunge his
knife to the heart of the victim, but the knife
drops from his nerveless hand, and the lamb,
no longer fettered, escapes. At the moment that
the expiring Saviour exclaimed, "It is finished,"
an unseen hand rent the veil of the Temple from
the top to the bottom. Thus God said, "I can
no longer reveal My presence in the Most Holy
Place." Type had met antitype in the death of
God's Son. The Lamb of God, slain from the
foundation of the world, is dead. The way into
the Holiest of all is laid open. A new and living
way, which has no veil between, is offered to
all. From henceforth all may walk in this way.
No longer need sinful, sorrowing humanity
await the coming of the high priest. It was as if a
living voice had spoken to the worshipers: There
is now an end to all sacrifices and offerings. The
Son of God has come according to His word,
"Lo, I come: in the volume of the book it is
written of Me, I delight to do thy will, O My
God" [Psalm 40:8]. "Behold the lamb of God,
which taketh away the sin of the world" [John
1:29]. – {12MR 416.3}*

Again, in case you missed it: *"A new and
living way, which has no veil between, is offered
to all."*

*"By the rending of the veil of the temple, God
said, I can no longer reveal My presence in the
most holy place. A new and living Way, before
which there hangs no veil, is offered to all. No
longer need sinful, sorrowing humanity await the
coming of the high priest".* – {5BC 1109.4}[8]

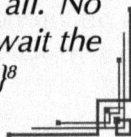

---

8   Within the Veil, pp. 2, 3.

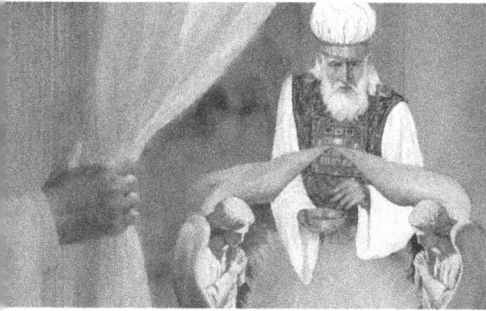

We answered the bulk of this argument under the first point, so we refer the reader to consider the justifications raised there prayerfully.

There is an idiom that says, "There are none so blind as those who will not see. The most deluded people are those who choose to ignore what they already know."; this saying has its roots in the Bible (see Jer. 5:21). It is an appropriate expression to use here because the second point under consideration notes Richards' awareness of the scriptural arguments. Nevertheless, he attempts to explain why they should be wholly ignored. He provides a mass of Scripture as justification to set aside what a plain "thus saith the Lord" clearly revealed respecting the throne of God in the Holy Place. They are used to undermine biblically established truth concerning the heavenly sanctuary and the atonement that is yet to be completed therein.

We will not belabor a point already covered satisfactorily; instead, we will turn our attention to the following argument raised in *Within the Veil*: that there is no veil (i.e., separation) between the Holy and Most Holy places of the heavenly sanctuary. While not a novel idea, it is an awkward argument to raise when the Scriptures used to substantiate it all denote that there is a veil, but we digress.

The reader should remember that when a type is changed or flawed, the truth it was designed to reveal is also damaged. David perceived that in the sanctuary, "every whit of it uttereth" God's glory (Ps. 29:9, margin). Paul later agreed (see Heb. 8:1ff.) that every aspect of the sanctuary was designed to glorify God and keep before His people the hope that one day, Christ would stand in the heavenly temple as their Advocate and High Priest. The psalmist further taught that God's "way" was in the sanctuary (Ps. 77:13), and in John's Gospel, Christ is that "way" (14:6). If our Lord—"the Way"—is "the same yesterday, and to day, and for ever" (Heb. 13:8; cf. James 1:17), would not a change in the antitype in any fashion mar

> *If our Lord—"the Way"—is "the same yesterday, and to day, and for ever" (Heb. 13:8; cf. James 1:17), would not a change in the antitype in any fashion mar "the way"? Shouldn't the truth that the Lord changes not (see Mal. 3:6) equally apply to the sanctuary designed to reveal His glory and salvific work?*

"the way"? Shouldn't the truth that the Lord changes not (see Mal. 3:6) equally apply to the sanctuary designed to reveal His glory and salvific work?

We repudiate the science of salvation the Lord taught through the types for thousands of years by asserting that there is no separation between the two apartments of the heavenly temple. God's insistence that they "make all things according to the pattern" (Heb. 8:5) and Moses "should make it according to the fashion that he had seen" (Acts 7:44) becomes a moot point then at best (see also Exod. 25:8, 9, 40; 1 Chron. 28:11-13). However, Scripture reveals a separation between the two apartments in the heavenly sanctuary (see Heb. 9:1-9, 24).

In order to enter the Holy Place of the earthly tabernacle, one had to enter through a veil or door (see Exod. 26:36, 37; 33:9, 10). That which separated the tabernacle's two apartments was also a veil or door (see 26:31-33; 1 Kings 6:16, 19-38; Isa. 6:1-4). These types meet their fulfillment in the heavenly antitypes, as depicted in John's vision when he saw "a door" opened (Rev. 4:1), revealing the Holy Place, and another opened (see 11:19) to reveal the Most Holy Place. He would again see the holiest of all opened, illustrating probation's close and the cessation of heavenly ministry on behalf of humanity (see 15:5). Revelation 11's account denotes the opening of the investigative judgment. In contrast, chapter 15 signifies its close—a solemn truth that can only be understood correctly by upholding the principle of type and antitype respecting the dual-apartment sanctuary.

There is ample proof given in the Scripture for a sanctuary above (see Jer. 17:12; cf. Ps. 11:4; 102:19; Hab. 2:20; Rev. 16:17), which is composed of two apartments (see Ps. 68:32-35; Heb. 8:1, 2; 9:8, 12, 24; 10:19). One author offered four sound biblical points that prove the heavenly sanctuary has two holy places:

> The following testimony on this point is conclusive. We gather it from the Old and New Testaments, that in the mouth of two or three witnesses every word may be established. 1) The tabernacle erected by Moses, after a forty-days' inspection of the one shown him in the mount, consisted of two holy places (Ex. 26:30-33), and is declared to be a correct pattern, or model, of that building (Ex. 25:8, 9, 40; cf. 39:32-43). But if the earthly sanctuary consisted of two holy places, and the great original, from which it was copied, consisted of only one, instead of likeness, there would be perfect dissimilarity. 2) The temple was built in every respect according

to the pattern which God gave to David by the Spirit (1 Chron. 28:10–19). And Solomon, in addressing God, says, "Thou hast commanded me to build a temple upon thy holy mount, and an altar in the city wherein thou dwellest, a resemblance of the holy tabernacle which thou hast prepared from the beginning" (Wis. 9:8). The temple was built on a larger and grander scale than the tabernacle; but its distinguishing feature, like the tabernacle, consisted in the fact that it was composed of two holy places (1 Kings 6; 2 Chron. 3). This is clear proof that the heavenly tabernacle contains the same. 3) Paul plainly states that "the holy places [plural] made with hands" "are the figures [plural] of the true." And the tabernacle, and its vessels, are "patterns of things in the heavens" (Heb. 9:23, 24). This is direct evidence that, in the greater and more perfect tabernacle, there are two holy places, even as in the "figure," "example," or "pattern." 4) The apostle actually uses the word holies (plural), in speaking of the heavenly sanctuary. The expression "holiest of all," in Heb. 9:8; 10:19, has been supposed by some to prove that Christ began to minister in the most holy place at his ascension. But the expression is not "hagia hagion," holy of holies, as in chapter 9:3; but is simply "hagion," holies. It is the same word that is rendered sanctuary in Heb. 8:2. In each of these three texts (Heb. 8:2; 9:8; 10:19), Macknight renders the word, "holy places." The Douay Bible renders it "the holies." And thus we learn that the heavenly sanctuary consists of two "holy places."[9]

A separating veil (i.e., door) teaches other essential, beautiful truths. We understand one of these truths in the veil's purpose. A veil covers or conceals the contents behind it (see Gen. 24:65; 38:14; Exod. 34:33–35; Num. 4:5; Isa. 25:7; 2 Cor. 3:13–16). The following quote illustrates this point better:

All who would enter the Sanctuary to worship, be he priest or penitent, must pass through the veil. The veil giving access to the court was twenty cubits wide and five high (Ex. 38:18). If cut in half, and the pieces stacked one above the other, they would form a square ten cubits to the side, the same as the two other veils.

---

9   John N. Andrews, The Sanctuary and Twenty-Three Hundred Days (Battle Creek, MI: Steam Press of the Seventh-day Adventist Publishing Association, 1872), p. 74.

While each was made of the same materials, and was similar in area and significance, they were designed so that the outermost one was broader and lower, and the inner ones narrower and higher. Did this suggest to the keen observer that the entry to the court, where justification by faith was provided, is the widest, and then, that as one moves on toward sanctification in the holy place, and on to glorification in the most holy, the "way" straitens as it approaches the throne …

The root of the Hebrew for veil (paroketh) means a hedge or screen, and connotes seclusion and protection.

These tapestries were only typical barriers, their fragile material designed as an invitation to enter. The Jewish commentator Rashi speaks of the veil as a screen between the King and His people; to provide Him with privacy, and them with an occasion to show respect (Pentateuch with Rashi's Commentary, I, pp. 143, 145).

The veils emphasize God's nearness, and signal that He wishes only a minimal screen to create mystery and arouse awe in His devotees …

The veil before the most holy place encouraged the priest who served in the first apartment to approach God's throne with confidence. Since the light of the Shekinah above the mercy-seat would have blinded, and perhaps destroyed him, the Lord veiled His glory. At the same time He granted His servant glimpses of His radiance through the interstices of its warp and weft …

Christ took human nature as a screen through which to display God's character to the universe. Paul explained that His humanity, "that is to say, His flesh" (Heb. 10:20) was symbolized by the veil of the Sanctuary. Prophecy revealed that "Christ was to come in 'the body of our humiliation' (Phil. 3:21, RV), 'in the likeness of men.' In the eyes of the world He possessed no beauty that they should desire Him; yet He was the incarnate God, the light of heaven and earth. His glory was veiled, His greatness and majesty were hidden, that He might draw near to sorrowful, tempted men" (DA, p. 23). "In the face of Jesus is the glory of self-sacrificing love" (DA, p. 20), and John "beheld His glory" by watching His every look and act as day by day (John 1:14) He displayed the nature of His Father. This exhibition will eventually attract "all," every being in the universe, to His luminous presence (John 12:32).

The Son of God joined His divinity with our humanity to become the Son of Man. Thus "veiled" the people might touch His person without fear as He moved among men (1 John 1:1–3; cf. Matt. 9:20, 21). His human body had especially been "fitted" (Heb. 10:5, margin) by the Godhead as Their Vehicle for this epiphany. By meditating on the life of Jesus each one of us today may see as much of the glorious truth about God's character as he or she is able to grasp.

Had the Son of God appeared with the glory which had been His with the Father before the world was created, "we could not have endured the light of His presence. That we might behold it and not be destroyed, the manifestation of His glory was shrouded. His divinity was veiled with humanity,—the invisible glory in the visible human form" (DA, p. 23) …

Let us come boldly to the throne of grace, the Palace curtain has been rent open, and Christ, as the glorious manifestation of God, will soon be revealed in His full majesty. Nineteen centuries ago this glorious consummation was dimly enacted. And throughout eternity the universe will never tire of gazing in awe and love upon the Reality of which the veil was such a beautiful yet subdued type. Jesus, through Whose flesh the character of God was revealed to mankind and all unfallen beings, will then have succeeded in drawing "all" to the Father. This accomplished, there will remain no trace of sin and rebellion, no blight of the curse or evidence of the fall. But in Christ's body of woman formed will forever remain the marks of the four nails in His hands and feet, and the scars of the spear in His side, and the thorn lacerations in His brow. These scars will be windows to glory for the universe. And there, it will be seen, remains forever the "secret of His power" (Hab. 3:4), the evidence of victory in the controversy between light and darkness. And there will glow ever more brightly the irrefutable proof that Light has finally triumphed.[10]

Oh, what sublime truths are revealed in the sanctuary's veils! Now, what about the quotes used by Richards from the pen of Ellen White used

---

10 Leslie Hardinge, With Jesus in His Sanctuary, 1st ed. (Harrisburg, PA: American Cassette Ministries, Book Division, 1991), pp. 75–78, 91, 92.

to sustain the view that there is no separation between the Holy and Most Holy places in the heavenly sanctuary? Here they are again for reference:

> All is terror and confusion. The priest is about to plunge his knife to the heart of the victim, but the knife drops from his nerveless hand, and the lamb, no longer fettered, escapes. At the moment that the expiring Saviour exclaimed, "It is finished," an unseen hand rent the veil of the Temple from the top to the bottom. Thus God said, "I can no longer reveal My presence in the Most Holy Place." Type had met antitype in the death of God's Son. The Lamb of God, slain from the foundation of the world, is dead. The way into the Holiest of all is laid open. A new and living way, which has no veil between, is offered to all. From henceforth all may walk in this way. No longer need sinful, sorrowing humanity await the coming of the high priest. It was as if a living voice had spoken to the worshipers: There is now an end to all sacrifices and offerings. The Son of God has come according to His word, "Lo, I come: in the volume of the book it is written of Me, I delight to do thy will, O My God" [Psalm 40:8]. "Behold the lamb of God, which taketh away the sin of the world" [John 1:29].[11]

> By the rending of the veil of the temple, God said, I can no longer reveal my presence in the most holy place. A new and living Way, before which there hangs no veil, is offered to all. No longer need sinful, sorrowing humanity await the coming of the high priest.[12]

Considering the above statements, was their intention to indicate that the antitype differed from the type or the heavenly temple does not contain dual apartments? Or have they been taken out of context, like were the Bible texts Richards offered to sustain such a theory? It is easy to find correlating statements that offer a clearer picture of Ellen White's point, all rooted in biblical truth.

> Through Christ the hidden glory of the holy of holies was to stand revealed. He had suffered death for every man, and by this

11   Ellen G. White, Manuscript Releases, vol. 12 (Silver Spring, MD: Ellen G. White Estate, 1990), p. 416.
12   Ellen G. White, "The Price of Our Redemption," The Youth's Instructor, June 21, 1900.

offering, the sons of men were to become the sons of God. With open face, beholding as in a glass the glory of the Lord, believers in Christ were to be changed into the same image, from glory to glory. The mercy seat, upon which the glory of God rested in the holiest of all, is opened to all who accept Christ as the propitiation for sin; and through its medium, they are brought into fellowship with God. The vail is rent, the partition walls broken down, the handwriting of ordinances canceled. By virtue of His blood the enmity is abolished. Through faith in Christ Jew and Gentile may partake of the living bread.[13]

Inspiration points us to the fact that when the veil was torn in half at the crucifixion of Christ, there was no longer "any secrecy there"; what was hidden by the emblematic veil is revealed now to all, both Jew and Gentile alike. That is the meaning when Ellen White said, "A new and living way, which has no veil between, is offered to all," and not that there is no separation of apartments in the heavenly sanctuary. Richards blatantly twisted the context of the quotes he cited.

---

13   Ellen G. White, *Letters and Manuscripts*, Lt 230., vol. 22 (Ellen G. White Estate, 1907).

When the apostle Paul wrote to the Hebrew believers that Christ went "within the veil" (See Hebrews 6:19, 20; 10:19, 20), it is obvious that the readers (who were Hebrews and not Gentiles) were familiar and acquainted with the Old Testament sanctuary services and types. Although he uses the language "second veil" in chapter 9:3, yet this is the only single instance in scripture where this phrase is used. In every single instance where the word "veil" is used in the Bible in connection with the sanctuary, without exception, it is only exclusively referring to the veil which separated the holy from the most holy place. And further, the phrase "within the veil" in every single instance in the Bible, without exception, only refers to entering into the most holy place. See Ex. 26:33; Lev. 16:2, 12, 15; Num. 18:7. Those are 5 witnesses that "within the veil" only refers to the most holy place. Furthermore, the phrase "without the vail" only refers to the work done by the priests in the holy place. See Ex. 26:35; 27:21; 30:6; 40:22, 26; Lev. 24:3. Thus we have at least 6 more witnesses to the fact that "without the vail" means the holy place, while "within the vail" can only refer to the most holy place. So no less than 11 witnesses agree with Paul's epistle to the Hebrews that "within the veil", whither Christ our forerunner has gone with his blood, was and is nothing less than entering into the very presence of God in the most holy place of the heavenly sanctuary, and that this was done by the time he wrote his epistle before his death in 68 AD.[14]

CONTENTION THREE: "WITHIN THE VEIL" MEANS IN THE MOST HOLY PLACE

14   Within the Veil, p. 3.

ere, Richards provides a detailed study of phrases "within the veil" and "without the vail"; both are points of reference for location within the sanctuary. By doing so, he upholds, to some extent, William Miller's fourth rule of Bible interpretation: to "bring all the scriptures together on the subject you wish to know, then let every word have its proper influence."[15] Unfortunately, that is as far as he goes, seemingly forgetting the part which states, "If you can form your theory without a contradiction, you cannot be in an error."[16] That part implies that even though one can gather a heap of scriptures to prove a point, one can use them to uphold an erroneous theory.

There is no need to expose all the contradictory points made by Richards throughout his paper, for the title itself refutes his entire theory. How can there be "no literal veil in heaven separating the holy and most holy places" if, by the very biblical evidence he supplied, Christ went "within the veil" (Heb. 6:19)? Perhaps, as he asserts, the veil is not "literal," leaving us with only two other options: a figurative or spiritual means of separation between the two apartments of the heavenly temple. Even if one believed the veil, as mentioned by the apostle Paul, was figurative or spiritual, wouldn't that still show a division like in the type and dismantle Richards' whole theory?

Then there is Miller's first rule, which emphasizes the importance of words and their context.[17] While it is true that "the only single instance in scripture" where the phrase "second veil" is used is by Paul in Hebrews (9:3), that does not change the fact that he used it—and used it to emphasize a point. It is a distinctive phrase crucial to grasping Paul's understanding of the heavenly sanctuary and the mediatorial work of Christ there. If there is a second veil, there must, of necessity, be a first; this is the obvious context of this "single instance in scripture," and simply dismissing its usage to establish one's theory is nothing more than "private interpretation" (2 Peter 1:20). Where does approaching the Bible in that manner end? Do we now question John's Gospel because much of what he records is not found in the other three Gospels?

---

15   Sylvester Bliss, Memoirs of William Miller (Boston: Joshua V. Himes, 1853), p. 70.
16   *Ibid.*
17   See *Ibid.*

Paul understood that Christ had to enter "within the veil" (Heb. 6:19) at His ascension. It is supposed that that veil is the one that leads into the Most Holy Place, but this is presumed by setting aside the words of the author and his contextual usage in favor of other Bible authors. If we allow Paul's words to stand as is in context with his entire epistle, then they make perfect sense. The veil that divides the Holy and Most Holy places is "the second veil" (9:1–5); therefore, there are two veils. The first of which he speaks "whither the forerunner is for us entered" (6:20) must be the first veil, which hung before the Holy Place and was called a "hanging" (Exod. 26:36, 37). When Jesus entered "within the veil," He entered the Holy Place of His tabernacle because that was its first apartment; and our hope, as an anchor of the soul, enters "within the veil" for the atonement of both apartments, including both the forgiveness and blotting out of sins.

Richards argues that if Paul used the phrase "within the veil" that way, he would be out of step with the other Bible writers. However, taking Hebrews as it reads offers substantial evidence that Paul perfectly agreed with what the Holy Spirit taught through other prophets. Their writings are "subject to" one another, for "God is not the author of confusion" (1 Cor. 14:32, 33). For example, Paul's account would align with John's in Revelation, where Christ is seen ministering in the Holy Place (see Rev. 1, 4, 8) before the way opened to the Most Holy (see 11:19; cf. Dan. 7:9, 10, 13).

Paul may be the only one to use the phrase "the second veil" in the Bible, but that does not invalidate its inspiration. Instead, it should encourage the reader to understand it in the context of Hebrews. Paul's "second veil" should be quantified by his use of the phrase "within the veil" (Heb. 6:19), which, as we have seen, refers to the door into the Holy Place, not the Most Holy. That understanding is in perfect agreement with Moses' singular usage of "within the vail" (Num. 18:7), indicating the sanctuary as a whole—Holy Place and Most Holy Place—when referring to the charge laid upon Aaron and his sons respecting the altar and tabernacle (see verses 5–7). Paul's usage of the phrase "within the veil," applied the way we have here, would be considered unorthodox if one follows Richards' reasoning but fits the literary style he used "in all *his* epistles ... in which are some things hard to be understood, which they that are unlearned and unstable wrest, as *they do* also the other scriptures, unto their own destruction" (2 Peter 3:16).

Christ, "being come an High Priest" of the "greater and more perfect tabernacle, not made with hands" (Heb. 9:11), as did the typical priests who entered the "figures" (verse 24) or "patterns" of the true—which are the "heavenly things themselves" (verse 23)—entered into "heaven itself" (verse

24). When He ascended to the right hand of the Father "in the heavens" (8:1), He became "a minister of the sanctuary and of the true tabernacle, which the Lord pitched, and not man" (verse 2)—the sanctuary of the "better [the new] covenant" (verse 6). Alternatively, as written in different translations, Christ became "a minister in the holy places" (8:2 ESV) or "of the holy places a servant" (YLT), correctly using the Greek word *hagion*, meaning "holies," translated as "sanctuary" in the Authorized Version.

Within the Veil contends that Jesus entered the Most Holy Place at His ascension. We have supplied enough evidence to the contrary should the reader wish to review; yet, because of a few texts in Hebrews, the objection is raised. Let us place two Bible translations in comparison to clarify the point further:

King James Version	Macknight Translation
The Holy Ghost this signifying, that the way into the holiest of all was not yet made manifest, while as the first tabernacle was yet standing. (Hebrews 9:8)	The Holy Ghost signifying this: that the way of the holy places was not yet laid open, while the first tabernacle still standeth. (Hebrews 9:8)
Neither by the blood of goats and calves, but by his own blood he entered in once into the holy place. (Hebrews 9:12)	Hath entered once into the holy places, not indeed by the blood of goats and of calves, but by his own blood. (Hebrews 9:12)
It was therefore necessary that the patterns of things in the heavens should be purified with these; but the heavenly things themselves with better sacrifices than these. (Hebrews 9:23)	There was a necessity therefore that the representations indeed of the holy places in the heavens, should be cleansed by these sacrifices; but the heavenly holy places themselves by sacrifices better than these. (Hebrews 9:23)
For Christ is not entered into the holy places made with hands, which are the figures of the true; but into heaven itself. (Hebrews 9:24)	Therefore Christ hath not entered into the holy places made with hands, the images of the true holy places but into heaven itself. (Hebrews 9:24)

King James Version	Macknight Translation
Having therefore, brethren, boldness to enter into the holiest by the blood of Jesus, By a new and living way, which he hath consecrated for us, through the veil, that is to say, his flesh. (Hebrews 10:19, 20)	Well then brethren having boldness in the entrance of holy places, by the blood of Jesus; which entrance he hath dedicated for us, a way new and living through the vail, that is his flesh (Heb. 10:19–20).

Now read Paul's description of these two holy places in either translation (Heb. 9:1–6) and see how clear and lucid Macknight makes these texts appear by comparing them with the pattern given to Moses. One thing remember [sic], that the two vails or doors open from the east, therefore it was morally impossible for any one to enter the second vail without passing the first, and then read carefully Heb. 9:6, 7, and it must be seen that neither high priest in the type or anti-type, could enter the Holiest of all first, or even have any service to perform there, until they had first ministered in the holy place. Every argument of Moses and Paul is right opposite to it. Why? It makes the shadow bottom upwards [sic] even to pass through the holy and go into the holiest first. The high priest could not go there until he had ministered in the holy one year; Jesus our high priest could not enter into the holiest in Heaven until he had finished his daily ministration and filled his Mediatorial office for all the world from AD 31 to AD 1844, 1813 ½ years.[18]

When compared to the totality of Scripture on this point, the argument raised in *Within the Veil*—namely, that Jesus went

> *When compared to the totality of Scripture on this point, the argument raised in Within the Veil—namely, that Jesus went directly into the Most Holy Place because there is no literal veil between the two apartments—falls hopelessly apart.*

---

18   Joseph Bates, [Bates' Pamphlet #3] An Explanation of the Typical and Anti-Typical Sanctuary by the Scriptures (Press of Benjamin Lindsey, 1850), p. 135.

directly into the Most Holy Place because there is no literal veil between the two apartments—falls hopelessly apart. The "faith once delivered unto the saints" (Jude 1:4) that has withstood the storm and tempest of others who have raised similar thoughts stands impervious to such a "wind of doctrine" (Eph. 4:14).

Before moving on to the following argument, another erroneous idea deduced from this third point is that when Paul, or any Bible writer, wrote in the affirmative, it meant the subject was either past or present reality. Richards introduced this when he wrote "that this [Christ entering the most holy place with his blood] was done by the time he [Paul] wrote his epistle before his death in 68 AD"[19] to close his argument. We will assume he is not intentionally setting forth a new Bible principle of interpretation here, but notwithstanding, is that idea even sound, or does it introduce a byway that will lead off the straight and narrow path? We disagree with the notion introduced in the closing thought of Point #3 in *Within the Veil* and offer a few examples to prove otherwise.

The apostle Paul wrote that God predestinated (i.e., foreordained) us to be "conformed to the image of his Son" (Rom. 8:29). This blessed will of God for us comes with three glorious realities that are not all experienced in real time: calling, justification, and glorification (see verse 30). These verses illustrate what any rational student of Scripture should understand: that Paul was using "the time past, for the time present, as the Hebrews use, who sometimes set down the thing that is to come, by the time that is past, to signify the certainty of it: and he hath also regard to God's continual working."[20] A Christian realizes that glorification comes at Christ's appearing (see Rom. 8:16–18; 2 Thess. 1:7–12) and would never even venture to claim perfection (see Job 9:20, 21), let alone glorification. Notwithstanding, Paul wrote that those "whom he did predestinate, them he also called: and whom he called, them he also justified: and whom he justified, them he also glorified" (Rom. 8:30) as present realities. Could it be that Paul understood that God's foreordination could be His present will, while the reality of it comes later, as Peter illustrated concerning the vicarious atonement of Christ (see 1 Peter 1:18–20)? Yes, of course, Paul did; he demonstrated that understanding in his knowledge of the sanctuary system (see Heb. 9:1–10:22).

Paul wrote that he and other living Christians would be "caught up together" with the resurrected righteous dead "in the clouds, to meet

---

19   Within the Veil, p. 3.

20   The Geneva Bible (Powder Springs, GA: Tolle Lege Press, 1599), Note on Romans 8:30.

the Lord in the air" (1 Thess. 4:17), yet he died, and the resurrection of the righteous at the second advent is still forthcoming. The antichrist was upcoming in the days of the apostles, yet they taught that the spirit of antichrist (the papacy) was already present in their day and actively working in the church long before the 1,260 years of papal supremacy and persecution (see 2 Thess. 2:6, 7; cf. 1 John 2:18; 4:3). Paul wrote that God "calleth those things which be not as though they were" (Rom. 4:17) in the context of Him making Abraham the father of many nations. In doing so, he referenced the covenant promise made by God to Abraham as a present reality (cf. Gen. 17:5), though Isaac was yet to be born—and before blessing Ishmael with an offspring of twelve princes (see verses 18–21). The Lord can inspire His messengers to write about upcoming events as presently taking place, though they would be fulfilled at a time appointed in the future.

These few simple examples demonstrate that the Bible is written in a style that puts future things as present realities to signify their certitude. Note that Paul, whose writings we used primarily in our examples due to his words being taken entirely out of context by brother Richards, kept in line with the other Bible writers regarding this writing fashion. Such literary styling is consistent with God Himself, who declares "the end from the beginning, and from ancient times the things that are not yet done" (Isa. 46:10). Understanding this concept will significantly aid the reader in seeing the discrepancies in the next point raised in *Within the Veil*.

Notice the following scriptures that clearly state that "we have received the atonement", have been "reconciled to God", have our sins "no more in remembrance", receive cleansing, etc, from the New Testament authors. Romans 5:10, 11; 2 Corinthians 5:18; Colossians 1:21; Hebrews 8:12; 10:16–18; 1 John 1:9. And that is only a few scripture references. The New Testament authors are clear that believers can have the assurance of salvation in Christ once faith is exercised in the "lamb of God which taketh away the sin of the world".

"In whom we have boldness and access with confidence by the faith of him." Ephesians. 3:12.

"And this is the record, that God hath given to us eternal life, and this life is in his Son. He that hath the Son hath life; and he that hath not the Son of God hath not life. These things have I written unto you that believe on the name of the Son of God; that ye may know that ye have eternal life, and that ye may believe on the name of the Son of God." 1 John 5:11–13.[21]

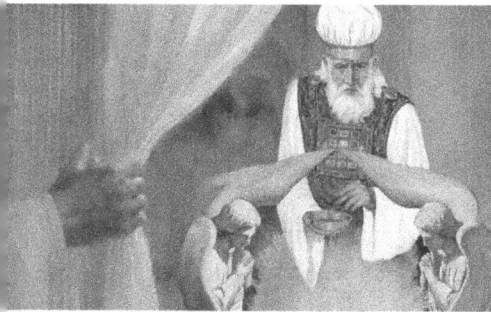

The beautiful truth of atonement within this argument is unfortunately squeezed by the erroneous premise addressed in the closing of our counterargument under Point #3. The error identified was that the writers of Scripture using past or present tenses when writing about a subject are contending for their present realities rather than for God's destined will. Unfortunately, this idea has biased Richards' understanding regarding the atonement. One should

---

21   Within the Veil, p. 3.

establish the context before making such a determination when reading the Scriptures, or they will find themselves on a byway leading to the ditch of private interpretation (see 2 Peter 1:20), as we have in Point #4.

While we believe Christ's offering of Himself was *complete* and sufficient—that nothing was wanting—that it was indeed a whole, ample atonement—we also believe, while respecting His sacrifice, that atonement was not *completed* on Calvary by that sacrifice itself. We believe the following summation is an accurate portrayal of how the Lord makes complete atonement:

> Important truths concerning the atonement are taught by the typical service. A substitute was accepted in the sinner's stead; but the sin was not canceled by the blood of the victim. A means was thus provided by which it was transferred to the sanctuary. By the offering of blood the sinner acknowledged the authority of the law, confessed his guilt in transgression, and expressed his desire for pardon through faith in a Redeemer to come; but he was not yet entirely released from the condemnation of the law. On the Day of Atonement the high priest, having taken an offering from the congregation, went into the most holy place with the blood of this offering, and sprinkled it upon the mercy seat, directly over the law, to make satisfaction for its claims. Then, in his character of mediator, he took the sins upon himself and bore them from the sanctuary. Placing his hands upon the head of the scapegoat, he confessed over him all these sins, thus in figure transferring them from himself to the goat. The goat then bore them away, and they were regarded as forever separated from the people.
>
> Such was the service performed "unto the example and shadow of heavenly things." And what was done in type in the ministration of the earthly sanctuary is done in reality in the ministration of the heavenly sanctuary. After His ascension our Saviour began His work as our high priest. Says Paul: "Christ is not entered into the holy places made with hands, which are the figures of the true; but into heaven itself, now to appear in the presence of God for us." Hebrews 9:24.[22]

---

22   Ellen G. White, The Great Controversy (Mountain View, CA: Pacific Press Publishing Association, 1911), p. 420.

That synopsis of the typical service perfectly agrees with what the Bible says on the subject (see Lev. 4, 16). There is the atoning sacrifice and then the atoning service. According to the type, complete atonement was made at the end of every year by the ministry of the high priest who served "unto the example and shadow of heavenly things" (Heb. 8:5). Teaching contrary to this explicit biblical model, such as promoted by Richards on his site, which says, "Seventh Day Baptists teach that Christ's atoning work was finished when He died on the cross,"[23] is an attack on the principle of type and antitype and the plan of salvation and suggests a counterfeit gospel (see Gal. 1:6–9).

Belief in complete atonement on and at the cross is not sustainable in the light of God's Word, making such a belief opinion rather than truth. Though many have taught it and congregations believe it, it is none the more real or sacred on that account if unsupported by Bible evidence.

1. If the atonement was made on Calvary, by whom was it made? The making of the atonement is the work of a Priest? but who officiated on Calvary?—Roman soldiers and wicked Jews.

2. The slaying of the victim was not making the atonement: the sinner slew the victim, Lev. 4:1–4, 13–15, etc., after that the Priest took the blood and made the atonement. Lev. 4:5–12, 16–21.

3. Christ was the appointed High Priest to make the atonement, and He certainly could not have acted in that capacity till after His resurrection, and we have no record of His doing any thing on earth after His resurrection which could be called the atonement.

4. The atonement was made in the Sanctuary, but Calvary was not such a place.

5. He could not, according to Heb. 8:4, make the atonement while on earth. "If He were on earth, He should not be a Priest." The Levitical was the earthly priesthood, the Divine, the heavenly.

6. Therefore, He did not begin the work of making the atonement, whatever the nature of that work may be, till after His ascension, when by His own blood He entered His heavenly Sanctuary for us.

---

23   "A Comparison of Seventh Day Baptists and Seventh-day Adventists," Independent Seventh Day Baptist Association, https://www.isdba.org/sdb-vs-sda (accessed January 2, 2020).

> *There is the atoning sacrifice and then the atoning service. According to the type, complete atonement was made at the end of every year by the ministry of the high priest who served "unto the example and shadow of heavenly things" (Heb. 8:5). Teaching contrary to this explicit biblical model, such as promoted by Richards on his site, which says, "Seventh Day Baptists teach that Christ's atoning work was finished when He died on the cross," is an attack on the principle of type and antitype and the plan of salvation and suggests a counterfeit gospel (see Gal. 1:6–9).*

Let us now examine a few texts that appear to speak of the atonement as passed. Rom. 5:11; "By whom we have now received the atonement," (margin, reconciliation). This passage clearly shows a present possession of the atonement at that time the apostle wrote; but it by no means proves that the entire atonement was then in the past.

When the Saviour was about to be taken up from His apostles, He "commanded them that they should not depart from Jerusalem, but wait for the promise of the Father," which came on the day of Pentecost when they were all "baptized with the Holy Ghost." Christ had entered His Father's house, the Sanctuary, as High Priest, and began His intercession for His people by "praying the Father" for "another Comforter", John 14:15, "and having received of the Father the promise of the Holy Ghost," Acts 2:33, He shed it down upon His waiting apostles. Then, in compliance with their commission, Peter, at the third hour of the day began to preach, "Repent, and be baptized every one of you in the name of Jesus Christ, for the remission of sins," Acts 2:38. This word remission, signifies forgiveness, pardon or more literally sending away of sins.

Now put by the side of this text another on this point from his discourse at the ninth hour of the same day, Acts 3:19, "Repent ye therefore; and be converted that your sins may be blotted out when the times of refreshing shall come from the presence of the Lord." Here he exhorts to repentance and conversion (turning away from sins); for what purpose? "That your sins may be (future) blotted out." Every one can see that the blotting out of sins does not take place at repentance and conversion; but follows, and must of necessity be preceded by them. Repentance, conversion, and baptism had then become imperative duties in the present tense; and when performed, those doing them "washed away" (Acts 22:16) remitted or sent away from them their sins. (Acts 2:28); and of course are forgiven and have "received the atonement"; but they had not received it entire at that time, because their sins were not yet blotted out.

How far then had they advanced in the reconciling process? Just so far as the individual under the law had when he had confessed his sin, brought his victim to the door of the tabernacle, laid his hand upon it and slain it, and the priest had with its blood entered the Holy and sprinkled it before the veil and upon the altar and thus made an atonement for him, and he was forgiven. Only that was the type, and this the reality. That prepared for the cleansing of the great day of atonement, this for the blotting out of sins "when the times of refreshing shall come from the presence of the Lord, and He shall send Jesus." Hence, "by whom we have now received the atonement" is the same as "by whom we have received forgiveness of sin." At this point the man is "made free from sin." The Lamb on Calvary's cross is our victim slain; "Jesus the Mediator of the new Covenant" "in the heavens" is our interceding High Priest, making atonement with His own blood, by and with which He entered there. The essence of the process is the same as in the "shadow". First, Convinced of sin; Second, Repentance and Confession; Third, Present the Divine sacrifice bleeding. This done in faith and sincerity we can do no more, no more is required.

Then in the heavenly Sanctuary our High Priest with his own blood makes the atonement and we are forgiven. 1 Peter 2:24; "Who His own self bare our sins in His own body on the tree." See also Matthew 8:17; Isaiah 53:4–12. His body is the "one sacrifice" for repenting mortals, to which their sins are imputed, and through whose blood in the hands of an active Priest they are conveyed to the heavenly Sanctuary. That was offered "once for all", "on the tree"; and all who would avail themselves of its merits must *through faith*, there receive it as theirs, bleeding at the hands of sinful mortals like themselves. After thus obtaining the atonement of forgiveness we must "maintain good works", not the "*deeds of the law*"; but "*being dead to sin should live unto righteousness.*" This work we all understand to be peculiar to the Gospel Dispensation.[24]

We agree that "believers can have the assurance of salvation in Christ once faith is exercised in the 'lamb of God which taketh away the sin of the world.'"[25] However, based on the conclusions drawn in this argument and the use of the word "assurance," Richards clearly misunderstands the word. Synonyms for assurance include the words "promise," "pledge," "guarantee," and "oath." None of them indicate the immediate reception of a thing but rather are like a check written out for payment. We may possess the promissory note, but its value is only as good as the fund from which it will be taken and predicated on us cashing it in. Holding a check written for $1 million does not make one a millionaire until it is cashed or the deposit clears, but it guarantees the money will be provided and the guarantor has the funds (see Eph. 1:11–14).

God is not a liar (see Num. 23:19; 1 Sam. 15:29; Titus 1:1–3; Heb. 6:11–20), and He promises salvation to the believer (see Rom. 10:8–10). However, this salvation, though promised, is the "end of [our] faith" to be "revealed in the last time" (1 Peter 1:9, 5). We are not "saved," as some put it—resting in a satisfied condition with no need to make advancement in the divine life the moment we accept Jesus as our Lord and Savior. The work is ongoing; there is no such thing as "once saved, always saved" (ref. Ezek. 18:24)[26]—a concept rife within Richards' fourth argument, whether intended or not.

24   Owen R. L. Crosier, The Sanctuary (Auburn, NY: Advent Review, 1850), pp. 17–20.
25   Within the Veil, p. 3.
26   See Ellen G. White, Christ's Object Lessons (Washington, D.C.: Review and Herald Publishing Association, 1900), pp. 154, 155; Selected Messages, book 1 (Washington, D.C.: Review and Herald Publishing Association, 1958), pp. 314, 315.

"Seventy weeks are determined upon thy people and upon thy holy city, to finish the transgression, and to make an end of sins, and to make reconciliation for iniquity, and to bring in everlasting righteousness, and to seal up the vision and prophecy, and to anoint the most Holy."

The word here used for "reconciliation" is the Hebrew word "kaphar", which is the identical word used in Leviticus 16 for "atonement". Therefore, according to Daniel's prophecy of the coming Messiah, Christ would bring "atonement for iniquity" and also "anoint the most holy" within the 70 weeks cut off from the 2300 days. The words "most holy" are the combined Hebrew words "qodesh qodesh" which taken combined only can refer to the most holy place of the sanctuary. It is a similar rendering in Hebrews 9:3 where the words "hagia hagion" are used to describe the "holiest of all" where the ark was placed. In fact, the Septuagint version uses this same phrase in Daniel 9:24 to describe the most holy which was anointed within the 70 weeks of Daniel's prophecy. In other words, according to this prophecy, Jesus Christ would offer himself as an offering for sin, to make "atonement for inquity", [sic] and enter the most holy place to present his blood for cleansing in the presence of God within the 70 weeks of the 2300 days. And the apostle Paul agrees with this when he writes the following: "For Christ is not entered into the holy places made with hands, which are the figures of the true; but into heaven itself, now to appear in the presence of God for us." Hebrews 9:24.[27]

---

27   Within the Veil., p. 4.

The faulty reasoning asserting that Paul's affirmative writing meant a present reality—an argument we covered in the third contention—is presented here again. Observe this when he wrote, "Jesus Christ would offer himself as an offering for sin, to make 'atonement for inquity,' [sic] and enter the most holy place to present his blood for cleansing in the presence of God within the 70 weeks of the 2300 days. And the apostle Paul agrees with this."[28] Our initial assumption was that this view of the Bible was not intentional; however, it appears to be coloring the pages of *Within the Veil*. Unfortunately, its author has forgotten how to color within the biblical lines.

Scripture teaches that reconciliation is a process ending with the Day of Atonement. First, "through the blood of his cross," Christ reconciled "all things unto himself" (Col. 1:20). Second, Christ became "a merciful and faithful high priest in things pertaining to God, to make reconciliation for the sins of the people" (Heb. 2:17). Finally, He performs the work of the high priest in the sanctuary above (see 8:1–6; 9:7–12) to "make an atonement for the holy sanctuary" and "for all the people" (Lev. 16:33). "For on that day shall the priest make an atonement for you, to cleanse you, that ye may be clean from all your sins before the LORD" (verse 30).

> Once again, Within the Veil mutilates the principle of type and antitype and, therefore, the truth it reveals. This mangling of truth is made even more egregious by claiming this as the fulfillment of the seventy-week prophecy (see Dan. 9:24), which is the key to understanding the 2,300 days (see 8:14).

This fifth argument bypasses the high priest's work as taught in the typical service (see Heb. 9:1–9), which Paul parallels with our heavenly High Priest (see 8:1–5). Once again, *Within the Veil* mutilates the principle of type and antitype and, therefore, the truth it reveals. This mangling of truth is made even more egregious by claiming this as the fulfillment of the seventy-week prophecy (see Dan. 9:24), which is the key to understanding the 2,300 days (see 8:14).

28   *Ibid.*
29   A day equals a year in Bible prophecy (see Num. 14:34; Ezek. 4:6), so 70 weeks—490 days—would equal 490 years.

There are six things delineated in this prophecy that are fulfilled during its 490 years,[29] the last of which was the anointing of "the most Holy" (Dan. 9:24). If we follow the biblical type, the anointing of the "most Holy" was the ceremony performed before the initiation of the sanctuary ministration, including both apartments and all their sacred vessels (see Exod. 40:9–11). The "most Holy" is the true tabernacle Christ, our High Priest, entered for us. Christ was to do in the true tabernacle in heaven what Aaron did in its pattern (see Heb. 6–9; cf. Exod. 30:22–30; Lev. 8:10–15).

Let us run through it all again to drive the point home:

The worldly sanctuary was the pattern of the true. "After the pattern of the tabernacle, and the pattern of all the instruments thereof, even so shall ye make it." "And look that thou make them after their pattern, which was showed thee in the mount." Ex. 25:9, 40. "And thou shalt rear up the tabernacle according to the fashion thereof which was showed thee in the mount." Chap. 26:30. "As it was showed thee in the mount, so shall they make it." Chap. 27:8. "According unto the pattern which the Lord had showed Moses, so he made the candlestick." Num. 8:4. "Our fathers had the tabernacle of witness in the wilderness, as he had appointed, speaking unto Moses, that he should make it according to the fashion that he had seen." Acts 7:44. "Who serve unto the example and shadow of heavenly things, as Moses was admonished of God when he was about to make the tabernacle; for, See (saith he) that thou make all things according to the pattern showed to thee in the mount." Heb. 8:5. "It was therefore necessary that the patterns of things in the Heavens should be purified with these; but the heavenly things themselves with better sacrifices than these. For Christ is not entered into the holy places made with hands, which are the figures of the true." Heb. 9:23, 24.

From these texts we learn two important facts: 1) We are many times certified that the tabernacle of witness was made according to the pattern which God showed to Moses. 2) That that pattern was a representation of the heavenly sanctuary itself. Heb. 8:2.

From Acts 7:45, we learn that the tribes of Israel carried the sanctuary with them into the promised land. In the book of Joshua it is called the house of God, or tabernacle; and we learn that it was set up at Shiloh. Josh. 9:23; 18:1; 19:51; Jer. 7:12. It is called "the Lord's tabernacle." Josh. 22:19. It is called "the sanctuary of the Lord." Chap. 24:26. In the book of Judges it is simply called "the house of God," located at Shiloh. Judg. 18:31; 20:18, 26, 31; 21:2. In 1 Samuel it is termed the "house of the Lord." Chap. 1:7, 24; 3:15. In chapters 1:9; 3:3, it is called "the temple of the Lord." In chapter 2:29, God calls it "my habitation," or tabernacle, margin. It still abode in Shiloh. Chap. 4:4. We now pass from the shadow to the substance. The typical sanctuary gave place to the true.

1. The sanctuary of the first covenant ends with that covenant, and does not constitute the sanctuary of the new covenant. Heb. 9:1, 2, 8, 9; Acts 7:48, 49.
2. That sanctuary was a figure for the time then present, or for that dispensation. Heb. 9:9. That is, God did not, during the typical dispensation, lay open the true tabernacle; but gave to the people a figure or pattern of it.
3. When the work of the first tabernacle was accomplished, the way of the temple of God in Heaven was laid open. Heb. 9:8; Ps. 11:4; Jer. 17:12.
4. The typical sanctuary and the carnal ordinances connected with it were to last only till the time of reformation. And when that time arrived, Christ came, an high priest of good things to come by a greater and more perfect tabernacle. Heb. 9:9–12.
5. The rending of the vail of the earthly sanctuary at the death of our Saviour, evinced that its services were finished. Matt. 27:50, 51; Mark 15:38; Luke 23:45.
6. Christ solemnly declared that it was left desolate. Matt. 23:37, 38; Luke 13:34, 35.
7. The sanctuary is connected with the host. Dan. 8:13. And the host, which is the true church, has had neither sanctuary nor priesthood in old Jerusalem the past 1800 years, but has had both in Heaven. Heb. 8:1–6.
8. While the typical sanctuary was standing, it was evidence that the way into the true sanctuary was not laid open. But when its services were abolished, the tabernacle in Heaven, of which it was a figure, took its place. Heb. 10:1–9; 9:6–12.
9. The holy places made with hands, the figures or patterns of things in the Heavens, have been superseded by the heavenly holy places themselves. Heb. 9:23, 24.

10. The sanctuary, since the commencement of Christ's priest-hood, is the true tabernacle of God in Heaven. This is plainly stated in Heb. 8:1–6. These points are conclusive evidence that the worldly sanctuary of the first covenant has given place to the heavenly sanctuary of the new covenant. The typical sanc-tuary is forsaken, and the priesthood is transferred to the true tabernacle.

But the most important question in the mind of the reader is this: How did Gabriel explain the sanctuary to Daniel? Did he not point out to him the transition from the "figure" or "pattern," to the "greater and more perfect tabernacle," the true holy places? We answer, He did.

1. Gabriel explained to Daniel what portion of the 2300 days belonged to Jerusalem and the Jews: "Seventy weeks have been cut off upon thy people, and upon thy holy city." - Whiting's Translation. Dan. 9:24. Then the whole of the 2300 days does not belong to old Jerusalem, the place of the earthly sanctu-ary, nor do they all belong to the Jews, the professed people of God in the time of the first covenant.

2. For in that period of seventy weeks, the transgression was to be finished; that is, the Jewish people were to fill up their measure of iniquity, by rejecting and crucifying the Messiah, and were no longer to be his people, or host. Dan. 9:24; Matt. 23:32, 33; 21:33–43; 27:25.

3. Gabriel showed Daniel that the earthly sanctuary would be destroyed shortly after their rejection of the Messiah, and never be rebuilt, but be desolate till the consummation. Dan. 9:26, 27.

4. The angel brings the new covenant to Daniel's view. "He [the Messiah] shall confirm the covenant with many for one week." Dan. 9:27; Matt. 26:28.

5. He brings to Daniel's view the new-covenant church, or host; viz., the "many" with whom the covenant is confirmed. Verse 27.

6. He brings to view the new-covenant sacrifice; viz., the cutting off of the Messiah, but not for himself, verse 26; and also the Prince, or Mediator, of the new covenant. Verse 25; 11:22; Heb.

12:24. He brings to Daniel's view the new-covenant sanctuary, and informs him that before the close of the seventy weeks, which belong to the earthly sanctuary, the most holy shall be anointed. That this "most holy" is the true tabernacle in which the Messiah is to officiate as priest, we offer the following testimony: "'And to anoint the most holy:' kodesh kodashim, the holy of holies."—Adam Clarke. Dan. 9:24.

"Seventy weeks are determined upon thy people, and the city of thy sanctuary that sin may be restrained, and transgression have an end; that iniquity may be expiated, and an everlasting righteousness brought in; that visions and prophecies may be sealed up, and the holy of holies anointed." - Houbigant's Trans. Dan. 9:24.

The fact is plain that of the vision of 2300 days concerning the sanctuary, only 490 pertained to the earthly sanctuary; and also that the iniquity of the Jewish people would, in that period, be so far filled up that God would leave them, and the city and sanctuary would soon after be destroyed, and never be rebuilt, but be left in ruins till the consummation. And it is also a fact that Gabriel did present to Daniel a view of the true tabernacle, Hebrews 8:1, 2, which, about the close of the seventy weeks, did take the place of the pattern. And as the ministration of the earthly tabernacle began with its anointing, so in the more excellent ministry of our great High Priest, the first act, as shown to Daniel, is the anointing of the true tabernacle or sanctuary, of which he is a minister. Exodus 40:9–11; Leviticus 8:10, 11; Numbers 7:1; Daniel 9:24.[30]

The anointing of the "most Holy" (Dan. 9:24) is crucial to understanding the heavenly sanctuary and its salvific services. Before anyone or anything, whether king, prophet, priest, the Messiah, or temple, could fulfill their divine purpose, they needed to be anointed (see Exod. 29:4–7; 40:1–35; 1 Sam. 16:11–13; 2 Sam. 5:1–4; 1 Kings 19:16; Luke 3:21–23; 4:18, 19; Acts 10:38). The Bible teaches there has always been a sanctuary in heaven (see Jer. 17:12), built before the pattern was shown to Moses in the mount (see Exod. 25:8, 9, 40; 1 Chron. 28:11–19; Heb. 8:5; 9:1–9, 23, 24). However, the purpose of the heavenly sanctuary, other than being a place for the Lord

30   James S. White, Bible Adventism (Battle Creek, MI: Seventh-day Adventist Publishing Association, n.d.), pp. 152–156.

to dwell (Exod. 15:17), did not go into effect until the coronation of its King-Priest (see Rev. 5; cf. Acts 2:1–4)[31] and its anointing (see Dan. 9:24; cf. Exod. 40:1–35). Furthermore, the function of the sanctuary was to handle the problem of sin (see Exod. 25:8; Lev. 16:29–34; Isa. 59:2), which could only be by promise until the actual death of the Lamb of God (see John 1:29, 36; Rev. 12:10, 11; cf. John 12:31–33).

Though last in order of existence, the earthly sanctuary was first in the ministry of atonement for sin. However, it "could not make him that did the service perfect, as pertaining to the conscience, which stood only in meats and drinks, and divers washings, and carnal ordinances" (Heb. 9:9, 10), which functioned as acted parables of those "good things to come, by a greater and more perfect tabernacle, not made with hands" (verse 11). "For Christ is not entered into the holy places made with hands, which are the figures of the true; but into heaven itself, now to appear in the presence of God for us" (verse 24).

31 See Ellen G. White, The Desire of Ages (Mountain View, CA: Pacific Press Publishing Association, 1898), p. 832; The Acts of the Apostles (Mountain View, CA: Pacific Press Publishing Association, 1911), p. 38.

The doctrine of the investigative judgment, as Seventh-day Adventists hold and teach it, was not fully formulated until at least 1857 and not in 1844, contrary to what we believe. James White first used the phrase "investigative judgment" in 1857 and formerly opposed Joseph Bates teaching this in 1845–51. Up until this time nothing of the sort was taught at all. In fact, the understanding of those disappointed in 1844 when Christ did not come was that Jesus had gone into the most holy place and shut the door of mercy forever on the world, and that only those Adventists who had believed William Miller's teachings were shut in with Christ and sealed in the most holy place in 1844. This was based on Samuel Snow's typology of the sanctuary which helped form the basis of the midnight cry, Hiram Edson's vision in the corn field, and O.R.L. Crosier's article in the Daystar laying out an argument of Christ's ministry in the most holy place based on the Old Testament types of the day of atonement. Incidentally, even the date of October 22 is suspect based on the testimony of history by both classical Jews as well as Karaites, that Yom Kippur took place in 1844 on September 23 and not October 22. But that is irrelevant at this point.

The point I am trying to make is that the day of atonement was a type to teach how God would remove sin from the believer in the offering provided, and not a judgment of investigation for the believer. There are several problems with the theology that SDAs teach in this regard. First, it is taught that sin is symbolically transferred to the sanctuary through the blood of sprinkling. But this is clearly not the case in the Bible. Sin pollutes God's sanctuary, while blood cleanses it. Blood never pollutes. See the following proofs that sin, and not the blood of sacrifices, pollutes God's sanctuary: 2 Chronicles 36:14; Psalm 106:38, 39; Jeremiah 34:15, 16; Zephaniah 3:14; Leviticus 16:16. So it is sin, and not blood, that pollutes God's sanctuary and God's holy name. In contrast, blood cleanses. See Leviticus 14:52; 16:15, 16, 19; Ezekiel 43:20–23; Hebrews 9:22.

It is evident, therefore, that it is the sins of God's people that defile the sanctuary, and not the blood of the sacrifice which God has provided as a way of escape from wrath and to cleanse the people from their sins. The question must be asked then, when did Christ offer His blood for cleansing as both sacrifice and priest to cleanse the people from their sins? Let us allow Paul to answer this question:

"And almost all things are by the law purged with blood; and without shedding of blood is no remission. It was therefore necessary that the patterns of things in the heavens should be purified with these; but the heavenly things themselves with better sacrifices than these. For Christ is not entered into the holy places made with hands, which are the figures of the true; but into heaven itself, now to appear in the presence of God for us: Nor yet that he should offer himself often, as the high priest entereth into the holy place every year with blood of others; For then must he often have suffered since the foundation of the world: but now once in the end of the world hath he appeared to put away sin by the sacrifice of himself. And as it is appointed unto men once to die, but after this the judgment: So Christ was once offered to bear the sins of many; and unto them that look for him shall he appear the second time without sin unto salvation." Hebrews 9:22–28.

The day of atonement, therefore, was a type of how Christ would offer his blood in atonement as both sacrifice and high priest for the sins of the people, and to provide a "new and living way" whereby the defiled consciences of men and women could be cleansed; for this is the clear meaning of the whole context of Hebrews 9 and 10 read together without any chapter breaks or divisions.[32]

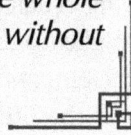

The main point of this argument is "that the day of atonement was a type to teach how God would remove sin from the believer in the offering provided, and not a judgment of investigation for the believer."[33] To this, we say yes and no. Yes, the typical Day of Atonement was to teach us how the Lord would remove sin; it was a yearly ceremony that was both cherished and feared due to the result of being either "cleansed" or "cut off" during that day (see Lev. 16:30; 23:27–31). However, Scripture does not endorse the conclusion that the Day of Atonement is void of an individual's review. How would the Lord determine who would be purified or eternally separated on that day if their lives were not examined? Regarding the Day of Atonement, the Jewish Encyclopedia states:

"God, seated on His throne to judge the world, at the same time Judge, Pleader, Expert, and Witness, openeth the Book of Records; it is read, every man's signature being found therein. The great trumpet is sounded; a still, small voice is heard; the angels shudder, saying, this is the day of judgment ... on the Day of Atonement it is sealed who shall live and who are to die ...."[34]

---

32   Within the Veil, pp. 4, 5.
33   *Ibid.*, p. 4.
34   Jewish Encyclopedia, s.v. "Atonement, Day of."

There is a principle used throughout the Bible: namely, enlargement through repetition, by which the Divine Teacher increases our knowledge (see Gen. 41:32; Job 33:14; Ps. 62:11; Dan. 2:1, 3); this is especially true in the book of Daniel. In chapter 2, there is given to the student of prophecy, via a dream, an outline of kingdoms from the days of Babylon to the setting up of God's kingdom (verses 37–44). Daniel's first vision, recorded in chapter 7, repeats this delineated line of kingdoms, adding additional information and introducing crucial elements, with the purpose of describing who will and will not make up the citizens of the kingdom of God.

The new elements in this enlarged-upon prophetic scheme are the introduction of the little horn, the judgment scene, and the giving of the kingdom to Christ (see verses 8–14). In Daniel' next vision (chapter 8), while following the same line of kingdoms and the subjects of said kingdoms, the focus of the student of prophecy is redirected to facilitate understanding. The introduction of ferocious beasts in chapter 7 (see verses 4–8) was to direct attention to the temporal aspects of the kingdoms of prophecy, while the use of sanctuary animals in chapter 8 (verses 3–12; cf. Ezek. 43:25) draws attention to their underlying religious nature. This change also influences the other subjects introduced in those respective chapters.

The judgment scene in Daniel 7 (verses 9, 10, 13, 14) supports the prophecy's predominant focus on statecraft, using words like "thrones," "judgment," "books," "dominion," "kingdom," etc. Aside from the Scriptures saying, "the judgment was set" (verse 10), the very act of thrones being "cast down" (verse 9) or "put in place" (NKJV) indicates judgment (see Ps. 9:7, 8; 122:5). The Bible gives a beautiful promise that "the saints of the most High shall take the kingdom, and possess the kingdom for ever, even for ever and ever" (Dan. 7:18), but there is not much given to show how they are deemed worthy of that kingdom in the vision. There is, however, a phrase pregnant with meaning that contains the elements on which chapter 8 will enlarge: namely, "Until the Ancient of days came, and judgment was given to the saints of the most High" (7:22).

God establishes the principle of repetition and enlargement through the dream of Daniel 2 and vision of Daniel 7, thus confirming its accuracy (see Gen. 41:32; Deut. 19:15; Matt. 18:16; John 8:17; 2 Cor. 13:1). After repeating the kingdoms of prophecy for the third time, now in language steeped in sanctuary themes, the vision of Daniel 8 opens before us the judgment, though calling it the cleansing of the sanctuary (see verse 14), uniting it to the Day of Atonement experience.

In Daniel 7, the coming of the Ancient of days (see verses 9, 13, 22) was His coming to judgment. For the sake of brevity, we will take liberties and assume the reader understands that it took place on October 22, 1844. Though given a quick jab in the sixth objection, that date has stood the test of time and criticism. Judgment being "given to the saints of the most High" (verse 22) means that "judgment was given for" (RSV) or "rendered in favor of" (NET) them. When the judgment began, it began for the people of God. Contrary to how *Within the Veil* presents it, judgment is not negative. Instead, "when we are judged, we are chastened of the Lord, that we should not be condemned with the world" (1 Cor. 11:32). The affliction and self-examination that is part of the Day of Atonement (see Lev. 16:29–31; Num. 29:7) is to keep one from further sin and reveal whether we are in the faith (see 2 Cor. 13:5). A people measured and chastened by the Lord (see Rev. 3:14, 19; 11:1) should ever keep in mind the purpose for such acts; the Lord "shall purify the sons of Levi, and purge them as gold and silver, that they may offer unto the LORD an offering in righteousness" (Mal. 3:3), that they "might be partakers of his holiness." (Heb. 12:10).

Within the Veil takes issue with sin being symbolically transferred into the earthly sanctuary through the blood sprinkled therein. That should be a simple matter to understand, but we will delve into it for clarity. The whole earthly sanctuary system was a model of the work of salvation that would be carried out in the heavens by the Lord; that is a fact that even brother Richards seeks to establish, albeit selectively.

When a man sinned, he brought his victim to the door of the tabernacle of the congregation to be offered up for himself. He laid his hand upon the head of the victim to denote that his sin was transferred to it (see Lev. 1–3). Then the victim was slain because of that transgression, and its blood, bearing that sin, guilt, and the power of forgiveness, was carried into the sanctuary and sprinkled upon it (see Lev. 4). Thus, this ministration went forward throughout the year. The people's sins were transferred from themselves to the victims offered in sacrifice and transferred through the blood of the sacrifices to the sanctuary itself. When the blood of the sacrifice was not sprinkled in the sanctuary, the priest would symbolically carry the sin into the sanctuary by eating a piece of the victim's roasted flesh (see 6:24–26; 10:17, 18). Both ceremonies equally symbolized the transfer of sin from the repentant soul to the sanctuary.

The argument says no, "sin pollutes God's sanctuary, while blood cleanses it."[35] We agree with the statement, but not with its conclusion; after

---

35   *Ibid.*

all, blood is both a defiler and a cleanser (see Num. 35:33). A record of sin was transferred into the sanctuary, not spiritually but figuratively, via the blood or flesh of the victim that bore the sin. If the sprinkled blood cleansed the sanctuary during the daily ministration (see Lev. 4), what was the purpose for the yearly ministration known as the Day of Atonement (see Lev. 16)? Why was there a need to "cleanse it, and hallow it from the uncleanness of the children of Israel" (verse 19) if, as the argument asserts, it was already made clean by the blood? Like most arguments in *Within the Veil*, this makes the sanctuary system questionable. It is more uncomplicated to understand that the sins of Israel were transferred to the sanctuary, and a special work became necessary for their removal: namely, the Day of Atonement, a name that signifies that atonement was experienced only by that yearly ministration.

Arguments such as the one under review echo the sentiment that the atonement was completed on the cross. However, this very thought undermines the types taught by the yearly feasts. There were seven feasts: four spring, three autumn (see 23:4–44). The first of the typical yearly feasts was Passover (see verses 4–8), which found its antitype in the death of "Christ our passover," who "is sacrificed for us" (1 Cor. 5:7). Next came the Feast of Unleavened Bread:

> It was not by chance that in the year the Saviour was crucified the Passover came on Friday, the sixth day of the week. Neither was it by, chance that the ceremonial Sabbath, the fifteenth day of Abib, came upon the seventh-day Sabbath of the Lord. It was type meeting antitype. The beloved disciple John, said, "That Sabbath was a high day," (Jn. 19:31) which term was used whenever the ceremonial annual Sabbath came upon the weekly Sabbath of the Lord.
>
> Four thousand years before, on the first sixth day of time, God and Christ finished the work of creation. God pronounced the finished work very good, and "He rested on the seventh day from all his work which He had made. And God blessed the seventh day, and sanctified it: because that in it He had rested from all His work which God created and made" (Gen. 2:2, 3). About twenty-five hundred years later, God, amid the awful grandeur of Sinai, commanded His people to "remember the Sabbath day, to keep it holy;" (Ex. 20:1–17) for upon that day—the seventh day—He rested from the work of creation.

It was a mighty work to speak this world into existence, to clothe it with verdure and beauty, to supply it with animal life, to people it with human beings made in the image of God; but it is a far greater work to take the earth marred by sin, its inhabitants sunken in iniquity, and re-create them, bringing them really to a higher state of perfection than when they first came from the hand of the Creator. This is the work undertaken by the Son of God; and when He cried upon Calvary, "It is, finished," He spoke to the Father, announcing the fact that He had complied with the requirements of the law, He had lived a sinless life. Christ, had shed His blood as a ransom for the world, and now the way was opened whereby every son and daughter of Adam could be saved if they would accept the offered pardon....

During the seven days following the Passover, the people ate unleavened bread. Seven, denoting a complete number, was a fitting type of the life that should be lived by the one who claims Christ as his Passover, and has the blessed assurance that his sins are covered by the blood of the Saviour. Leaven is a type of "malice and wickedness" unleavened bread represents "sincerity and truth" (1 Cor. 5:8). He who's past sins are hidden (Rom. 4:7,8), and who realizes what it is to have the condemnation of his old life lifted from him, enters into a new life, and should not return to his life of sin, but live in all "sincerity and truth." All this was symbolized by the seven day Feast of Unleavened Bread, following the Passover....

The offering of first-fruits came on the third day of the Passover feast. The fourteenth day of the month Abib, or Nisan, the Passover was eaten, the fifteenth day was the Sabbath, and upon the sixteenth day, or as the Bible states it, "On the morrow after the Sabbath," the first-fruits were waved before the Lord (Lev. 23:5–11)....

The waving of the first-fruits was the principal service of the day, but a lamb was also offered as a burnt-offering. No portion of the first-fruits were ever burned in the fire, for they were a type of resurrected beings clad in immortality, nevermore subject to death or decay.

... On the sixteenth day of the month, in the year the Saviour died, the Jews in the temple God had forsaken went through the empty form of offering the heads of grain, while Christ, the antitype, arose from the dead, and became "the first-fruits of them that slept" (1 Corinthians 15:20). Type had met antitype.

Every field of ripened grain gathered into the garner, is but a reminder of the great final harvest, when the Lord of the harvest, with His band of angel reapers, will come to gather the spiritual harvest of the world. Just as the first handful of grain was a pledge of the coming harvest, so the resurrection of Christ was a pledge of the resurrection of the righteous; "for if we believe that Jesus died and rose again, even so them also which sleep in Jesus will God bring with Him" (1 Thess. 4:14).

The priest did not enter the temple with only one head of grain, he waved a handful before the Lord; neither did Jesus come forth from the grave alone, for "many bodies of the saints which slept arose, and came out of the graves after His resurrection" (Matt. 27:52, 53). While the Jews were preparing to perform the empty service of the offering of first-fruits in the temple, and the Roman soldiers were telling the people that the disciples had stolen the body of Jesus, these resurrected saints went through the streets of the city, proclaiming that Christ had indeed risen (Matt. 28:11–15; cf. Eph. 4:8, margin).[36]

The final spring feast held in the first half of the year was Pentecost, thus named because it was held fifty days after the waving of the first fruits (see Lev. 23:16). This feast was also called the Feast of Weeks due to the seven weeks occurring between it and the Passover feast (see Exod. 23:14–16). Pentecost met its antitype when the disciples "were all with one accord in one place" and "filled with the Holy Ghost, and began to speak with other tongues, as the Spirit gave them utterance" (Acts 2:1, 4).

All the feasts, as mentioned above, were fulfilled without fail. Since "God is not the author of confusion" (1 Cor. 14:33), the autumn feasts should also find historical fulfillment. The typical Feast of Trumpets, sounding ten days before the Day of Atonement (see Num. 29:1) to warn Israel of the event's near approach, found its antitype in the judgment-hour message (see Rev. 14:6, 7) given ten years before the judgment began.[37] The Day of Atonement, attacked

---

36   *The Cross and Its Shadow*, pp. 104–106, 108–110.

37   "From 1834 on until the great Disappointment in the autumn of 1844, there was scarcely a pause in Miller's public proclamation of Christ's soon coming, which was always presented in the setting of the prophecies" (LeRoy Edwin Froom, *The Prophetic Faith of Our Fathers*, vol. 4 [Washington, D.C.: Review and Herald Publishing Association, 1954], p. 510; see also pp. 493–496).

by the current point under evaluation, found its antitypical fulfillment in the investigative judgment that commenced in 1844.

Within the Veil leads us to conclude that the atonement found its fulfillment on Calvary. However, that supposition amalgamates the Passover held on "the fourteenth day of the first month" (Lev. 23:5), "the month of Abib" (Deut. 16:1), with the Day of Atonement held "in the seventh month, on the tenth day of the month" (Lev. 16:29), "the month Ethanim" (1 Kings 8:2). If people believe that contortion of time and Scripture, then God has sent "them strong delusion, that they should believe a lie" (2 Thess. 2:11; cf. verses 10, 12). The Day of Atonement cannot fall upon the feast of Passover; an assumption such as that undercuts the type.

The apostle Paul states the fact of the cleansing of the earthly and the heavenly sanctuaries, and plainly affirms that the latter must be cleansed for the same reason that the former had been. He speaks as follows: "And almost all things are by the law purged with blood; and without shedding of blood is no remission. It was therefore necessary that the patterns of things in the heavens should be purified with these; but the heavenly things themselves with better sacrifices than these. For Christ is not entered into the holy places made with hands, which are the figures of the true; but into Heaven itself, now to appear in the presence of God for us." Heb. 9:22–24. Two important facts are stated in this portion of Scripture. 1) The earthly sanctuary was cleansed by blood. 2) The heavenly sanctuary must be cleansed by better sacrifice, that is, by the blood of Christ....

These words, as rendered by Macknight, are very clear: "And almost all things, according to the law, are cleansed with blood, and

> **66**
>
> *Within the Veil leads us to conclude that the atonement found its fulfillment on Calvary. However, that supposition amalgamates the Passover held on "the fourteenth day of the first month" (Lev. 23:5), "the month of Abib" (Deut. 16:1), with the Day of Atonement held "in the seventh month, on the tenth day of the month" (Lev. 16:29), "the month Ethanim" (1 Kings 8:2). If people believe that contortion of time and Scripture, then God has sent "them strong delusion, that they should believe a lie" (2 Thess. 2:11; cf. verses 10, 12).*
>
> **99**

without the shedding of blood, there is no remission. There was a necessity, therefore, that the representations indeed of the holy places in the heavens should be cleansed by these sacrifices; but the heavenly holy places themselves, by sacrifices better than these. Therefore Christ hath not entered into the holy places made with hands; the images of the true holy places; but into heaven itself, now to appear before the face of God, on our account." Heb. 9:22–24. Then the fact of the cleansing of the heavenly sanctuary is plainly taught by the apostle Paul in his commentary on the typical system. And this great truth, plainly stated, is worthy of lasting remembrance.

By many, the idea of the cleansing of the heavenly sanctuary will be treated with scorn, "because," say they, "there is nothing in Heaven to be cleansed." Such overlook the fact that the holy of holies, where God manifested his glory, and which no one but the High Priest could enter, was, according to the law, to be cleansed, because the sins of the people were borne into it by the blood of sin-offering. Lev. 16. And they overlook the fact that Paul plainly testifies that the heavenly sanctuary must be cleansed for the same reason. Heb. 9:23, 24. See also Col. 1:20. It was unclean in this sense only: the sins of men had been borne into it through the blood of sin offering, and they must be removed. This fact can be grasped by every mind.

The work of cleansing the sanctuary changes the ministration from the holy place to the holiest of all. Lev. 16; Heb. 9:6, 7; Rev. 11:19. As the ministration in the holy place of the temple in heaven began immediately after the end of the typical system, at the close of the sixty-nine and a half weeks (Dan. 9:27), so the ministration in the holiest of all, in the heavenly sanctuary, begins with the termination of the 2300 days. Then our High Priest enters the holiest to cleanse the sanctuary. The termination of this great period marks the commencement of the ministration of the Lord Jesus in the holiest of all. This work, as presented in the type, we have already seen was for a two-fold purpose, viz.: the forgiveness of iniquity, and the cleansing of the sanctuary. And this great work our Lord accomplishes with his own blood; whether by the actual presentation of it, or by virtue of its merits, we need not stop to inquire.[38]

38   The Sanctuary and Twenty-Three Hundred Days, pp. 88–91.

As long as the first tabernacle stood there was also an earthy priesthood, along with earthly sacrifices, under the first or old covenant whereby people approached unto God and showed their faith in the coming sacrifice that God would provide. But it is evident that once the true sacrifice arrived in earth's history that a "new and living way" to God would be opened to all through faith in Christ as "the lamb of God which taketh away the sin of the world". Thus the writer of Hebrews lays out the argument that Jesus is of a different order of priesthood "after the order of Melchizedek" and not of Levi, "of a greater and more perfect tabernacle", "which the Lord pitched, and not man".

So when did the earthly tabernacle lose its significance and a "new living way" open to all? When was the way into "the holiest of all" made manifest?

"All is terror and confusion. The priest is about to plunge his knife to the heart of the victim, but the knife drops from his nerveless hand, and the lamb, no longer fettered, escapes. At the moment that the expiring Saviour exclaimed, "It is finished," an unseen hand rent the veil of the Temple from the top to the bottom. Thus God said, "I can no longer reveal My presence in the Most Holy Place." Type had met antitype in the death of God's Son. The Lamb of God, slain from the foundation of the world, is dead. The way into the Holiest of all is laid open. A new and living way, which has no veil between, is offered to all. From henceforth all may walk in this way. No longer need sinful, sorrowing humanity await the coming of the high priest. It was as if a living voice had spoken to the worshipers: There is now an end to all sacrifices and offerings. The Son of God has come according to His word, "Lo, I come: in the volume of the book it is written of Me, I delight to do thy will, O My God" [Psalm 40:8]. "Behold the lamb of God, which taketh away the sin of the world" [John 1:29]. – {12MR 416.3}.[39]

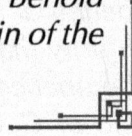

Richards said, "the writer of Hebrews lays out the argument that Jesus is of a different order of priesthood 'after the order of Melchizedek' and not of Levi, 'of a greater and more perfect tabernacle,' 'which the Lord pitched, and not man.'"[40] That is true, but like all the statements with which we have previously agreed in *Within the Veil*, the statements may be accurate, but their conclusions contain serious errors. This point, while leading the reader back to one of the leading arguments respecting the absence of any separation in the heavenly sanctuary, introduces the idea that the heavenly tabernacle operates by a different set of rules and principles from its earthly type. Therefore, using the earthly type as an example does not fit. With that idea in place, people can wrest the Scriptures in any way that pleases them; however, the Bible clarifies what is different and what is similar between the earthly and heavenly systems.

The apostle Paul introduces Christ as our "great high priest, that is passed into the heavens" (Heb. 4:14) and draws a beautiful parallel between Him and His earthly representatives (see 5:1–10). He picks up that theme again, this time drawing a comparison between Christ and Melchizedek (see 6:19–7:3). Here, "there is made of necessity a change also of the law" (7:12) because there was a change of the priesthood (see verses 13–25, 28). Note that the change pertained to the law respecting the priesthood's lineage, not to the priest's ministration; that is key. There is a difference in the ministration of our High Priest and the earthly priests mentioned

---

39   Within the Veil, pp. 5, 6.
40   *Ibid.*, p. 5.

concerning the frequency of the sin offering. However, Paul clearly emphasizes that there was an offering for sin made by Christ nevertheless (see verses 26, 27), and he will show that it followed the earthly example.

In Hebrews 8, Paul brings together the sanctuary's type and antitype (see verses 1–5) through the old and new covenants (see verses 6–13). The careful reader will notice that Paul never makes the case that the heavenly sanctuary is structurally different from the earthly or that the ministration of our heavenly High Priest is different from the earthly. Instead, he uses the earthly to explain the heavenly as the principle of type and antitype demands. When Paul wrote, "Who serve unto the example and shadow of heavenly things" (verse 5), the context of that statement covers not only the priests (see verses 3, 4) but also the sanctuary (see verse 2) and its furniture. We understand that by his reference to the command given to Moses: "See, saith he, that thou make all things according to the pattern shewed to thee in the mount" (verse 5; cf. Exod. 25:40).

Paul now highlights the first (i.e., old) covenant and its earthly sanctuary and services (see Heb. 9:1–7), then, in plain language, says they were "a figure for the time then present" (verse 9). Different Bible versions translate that phrase as "It was symbolic for the present time" (NKJV), "an illustration for the present time" (NIV), "a parable" (DRA), "a symbol" (NET), "an example" (GW), and "a simile in regard to the present time" (YLT). Since the earthly sanctuary and its ministration are thus described, the reader must inquire, "What did those patterns illustrate?" Paul replies, "The patterns of things in the heavens ... For Christ is not entered into the holy places made with hands, *which are* the figures of the true; but into heaven itself, now to appear in the presence of God for us" (verses 23, 24).

Not once, in all of Hebrews, does Paul give credence to the idea that the heavenly sanctuary or its services were different from their earthly "figures," aside from the evident and necessary changes he listed. Pulling the "Melchizedek card" is a sorry

> **—❝—**
> *Not once, in all of Hebrews, does Paul give credence to the idea that the heavenly sanctuary or its services were different from their earthly "figures," aside from the evident and necessary changes he listed. Pulling the "Melchizedek card" is a sorry attempt by brother Richards to introduce a thought that is far from biblical and even destroys his previous arguments interwoven with the type-and-antitype principle.*
> **—❞—**

attempt by brother Richards to introduce a thought that is far from biblical and even destroys his previous arguments interwoven with the type-and-antitype principle.

This contention with Point #7 touches on an essential truth regarding the "new and living way" (10:20) opened for us by the death of the Son of God, but what is this different channel opened by Christ whereby we can draw near to the Lord? *Within the Veil* uses this beautiful truth in a manner that gives the understanding that the new way was a route devoid of a veil, undermining the context of the salvational truth taught by Paul.

> Perfection in every respect is attained through the priesthood, the sacrifice, and the service of this our great High Priest at the right hand of the throne of the Majesty in the heavens in His ministry in the sanctuary and the true tabernacle, which the Lord pitched, and not man. "Whereof the Holy Ghost also is a witness to us: for after that He had said before, this is the covenant that I will make with them after those days, saith the Lord, I will put My laws into their hearts, and in their minds will I write them; and their sins and iniquities will I remember no more. Now where remission of these is, there is no more offering for sin." Hebrews 10:15–18.
>
> And this is the "new and living way" which Christ, through the flesh, "hath consecrated for us"—for all mankind—and by which every soul may enter into the holiest of all—the holiest of all places, the holiest of all experiences, the holiest of all relationships the holiest of all living. This new and living way He "hath consecrated for us through the flesh;" that is, He, coming in the flesh, identifying Himself with mankind in the flesh, has, for us who are in this flesh, consecrated a way from where we are to where He now is, at the right hand of the throne of the Majesty in the heavens in the holiest of all.
>
> In His coming in the flesh—having been made in all things like unto us and having been tempted in all points like as we are—He has identified Himself with every human soul just where that soul is. And from the place where every human soul is, He has consecrated for that soul a new and living way through all the vicissitudes and experiences of a whole lifetime, and even through death and the tomb, into the holiest of all at the right hand of God for evermore.
>
> O that consecrated way! Consecrated by His temptations

and sufferings, by His prayers and tears, by His holy living and sacrificial dying, by His triumphant resurrection and glorious ascension, and by His triumphal entry into the holiest of all, at the right hand of the throne of the Majesty in the heavens!

And this "way" He has consecrated for us. He, having become one of us, has made this way our way; it belongs to us. He has endowed every soul with divine right to walk in this consecrated way, and by His having done it Himself in the flesh—in our flesh— He has made it possible, yea, He has given actual assurance, that every human soul can walk in that way, in all that that way is and by it enter fully and freely into the holiest of all.

He, as one of us, in our human nature, weak as we, laden with the sins of the world, in our sinful flesh, in this world, a whole lifetime, lived a life "holy, harmless, undefiled, separate from sinners," and "was made" and ascended "higher than the heavens." And by this He has made and consecrated a way by which, in Him, every believer can in this world and for a whole lifetime, live a life holy, harmless, undefiled, separate from sinners and as a consequence be made with Him higher than the heavens.[41]

If one looks at this passage with more than a surface glance, one would understand that the "new and living way" is not Christ's flesh in place of a veil; rather, His flesh is what enables us to enter through the veil. Both James White and Uriah Smith explain it as follows:

Question: Please explain Hebrews 10:20. How is Christ's flesh the vail?

Answer: It isn't. The difficulty arises from this misunderstanding of the text. Verses 19 and 20 read as follows: "Having therefore, brethren, boldness to enter into the holiest (holies) by the blood of Jesus, by a new and living way which he hath consecrated for us, through the vail, that is to say, his flesh." What is his flesh? Not the vail, but the way. A little transposition of terms will show more plainly this idea; thus, "By a new and living way, that is to say, his flesh, which he hath consecrated for us through the vail." How is his flesh a way through the vail? Because it is by his offering of himself

---

41   Alonzo T. Jones, The Consecrated Way to Christian Perfection (Mountain View, CA: Pacific Press Publishing Company, 1905), pp. 82, 83.

that we gain access there. Paul says, Hebrews 9:12, that "by his own blood he entered in once (Gr. once for all) into the holy place" (Gr. plural, holy places). And it is by his sacrifice, his blood, that we also find entrance there. With this understanding of the text it is consistent with other scriptures, and the figure is a beautiful one; but with the other view it is involved in unexplainable inconsistencies and difficulties; for we might well inquire, in the language of the question, how his flesh could be the vail; and, in that case, what is the new and living way?[42]

Once again, now the third time, an attempt is made to bolster the mistaken idea of no veil between the Holy and Most Holy places of the heavenly sanctuary by quoting Ellen White. The slant placed upon her words is a gross misapplication of the "new and living way, which has no veil between" that "is offered to all."[43] When we compare her statement with others in her writings, the beauty of truth shines through the foulness of error and exploitation.

Christ was nailed to the cross between the third and sixth hour, that is, between nine and twelve o'clock. In the afternoon He died. This was the hour of the evening sacrifice. Then the veil of the temple, that which hid God's glory from the view of the congregation of Israel, was rent in twain from top to bottom.

Through Christ the hidden glory of the holy of holies was to stand revealed. He had suffered death for every man, and by this offering the sons of men were to become the sons of God. With open face, beholding as in a glass the glory of the Lord, believers in Christ were to be changed into the same image, from glory to glory. The mercy seat, upon which the glory of God rested in the holiest of all, is opened to all who accept Christ as the propitiation for sin, and through its medium, they are brought into fellowship with God. The veil is rent, the partition walls broken down, the handwriting of ordinances canceled. By virtue of His blood the enmity is abolished. Through faith in Christ Jew and Gentile may partake of the living bread.[44]

---

42   Uriah Smith, The Biblical Institute (Oakland, CA: Pacific Seventh-day Adventist Publishing House, 1878), p. 75.
43   Manuscript Releases, vol, 12, p. 416.
44   Letters and Manuscripts, vol. 22.

It was not the hand of the priest that rent from top to bottom the gorgeous veil that divided the holy from the most holy place. It was the hand of God. When Christ cried out, "It is finished," the Holy Watcher that was an unseen guest at Belshazzar's feast pronounced the Jewish nation to be a nation unchurched. The same hand that traced on the wall the characters that recorded Belshazzar's doom and the end of the Babylonian kingdom, rent the veil of the temple from top to bottom, opening a new and living way for all, high and low, rich and poor, Jew and Gentile. From henceforth people might come to God without priest or ruler.[45]

When Christ on the cross cried out, "It is finished," the veil of the temple was rent in twain. This veil was significant to the Jewish nation. It was of most costly material, of purple and gold, and was of great length and breadth. At the moment when Christ breathed His last, there were witnesses in the temple who beheld the strong, heavy material rent by unseen hands from top to bottom. This act signified to the heavenly universe, and to a world corrupted by sin, that a new and living way had been opened to the fallen race, that all sacrificial offerings terminated in the one great offering of the Son of God. He who had hitherto dwelt in the temple made with hands, had gone forth never again to grace it with His presence.[46]

God did not lessen His claim upon men in order to save them. When as a sinless offering Christ bowed His head and died, when by the Almighty's unseen hand the veil of the temple was rent in twain, a new and living way was opened. All can now approach God through the merits of Christ. It is because the veil has been rent that men can draw nigh to God. They need not depend on priest or ceremonial sacrifice. Liberty is given to all to go directly to God through a personal Saviour.[47]

45   Manuscript Releases, vol. 12, p. 392.
46   "Our Sacrifice," The Signs of the Times, December 8, 1898.
47   The SDA Bible Commentary, vol. 7 (Washington, D.C.: Review and Herald Publishing Association, 1957), p. 932.

When Christ died upon the cross of Calvary, a new and living way was opened to both Jew and Gentile. The Saviour was henceforth to officiate as Priest and Advocate in the heaven of heavens. Henceforth the blood of beasts offered for sins was valueless, for the Lamb of God had died for the sins of the world.[48]

Anciently believers were saved by the same Saviour as now, but it was a God veiled. They saw God's mercy in figures... Christ's sacrifice is the glorious fulfillment of the whole Jewish economy... When as a sinless offering Christ bowed His head and died, when by the Almighty's unseen hand the veil of the temple was rent in twain, a new and living way was opened. All can now approach God through the merits of Christ. It is because the veil has been rent that men can draw nigh to God. They need not depend on priest or ceremonial sacrifice. Liberty is given to all to go directly to God through a personal Saviour.[49]

God grants men a probation in this world, that their principles may become firmly established in the right, thus precluding the possibility of sin in the future life, and so assuring the happiness and security of all. Through the atonement of the Son of God alone could power be given to man to establish him in righteousness, and make him a fit subject for heaven. The blood of Christ is the eternal antidote for sin. The offensive character of sin is seen in what it cost the Son of God in humiliation, in suffering and death. All the worlds behold in him a living testimony to the malignity of sin, for in his divine form he bears the marks of the curse. He is in the midst of the throne as a Lamb that hath been slain. The redeemed will ever be vividly impressed with the hateful character of sin, as they behold Him who died for their transgressions. The preciousness of the Offering will be more fully realized as the blood-washed throng more fully comprehend how God has made a new and living way for the salvation of men, through the union of the human and the divine in Christ.[50]

---

48   The SDA Bible Commentary, vol. 7A (Washington, D.C.: Review and Herald Publishing Association, 1970), p. 487.
49   God's Amazing Grace (Washington, D.C.: Review and Herald Publishing Association, 1973), p. 155.
50   "What Was Secured by the Death of Christ," The Signs of the Times, December 30, 1889.

The privileges that God has given us, the advantages that He has bestowed, the promises that He has made, should inspire us, with far greater zeal and devotion. "God so loved the world, that He gave His only-begotten Son, that whosoever believeth in Him should not perish, but have everlasting life." Christ came to this world to live and die for sinners. He bids His disciples put forth untiring effort for those who know not the joy of communion with Him. He stands ready to give them power for the fulfilment of the commission.

The veil has been rent from top to bottom. A new and living way has been opened. And now, all who will may reach forth their hands unto God, and take hold of His strength, and they shall make peace with Him. The heathen world is no longer to be wrapped in darkness. The gloom of superstition is to disappear before the bright beams of the Sun of Righteousness. The powers of hell have been overcome. The truth of the words has been proven, "I am sought of them that asked not for Me; I am found of them that sought Me not; I said, Behold Me, behold Me, unto a nation that was not called by My name."

Go, teach and preach Christ. Instruct and educate all who know not of His grace, His goodness, and His mercy. Teach the people. "How then shall they call on Him in whom they have not believed? and how shall they believe in Him of whom they have not heard? and how shall they hear without a preacher?"

"How beautiful upon the mountains are the feet of him that bringeth good tidings, that publisheth peace; that bringeth good tidings of good, that publisheth salvation; that saith unto Zion, Thy God reigneth! ... Break forth into joy, sing together, ye waste places of Jerusalem; for the Lord hath comforted His people, He hath redeemed Jerusalem. The Lord hath made bare His holy arm in the eyes of all the nations, and all the ends of the earth shall see the salvation of our God."[51]

The priesthood itself had become corrupt. Priest after priest filled his appointment and performed his religious duties as an actor in a theater. Christ was fully aware of the high priest's unworthiness to occupy the position that he did. He knew that he had not

---

51   "Power for Service," The Signs of the Times, August 19, 1903.

the character that would enable God to connect with him. But knowing all this, Christ responded. The true High Priest stood before the false priest, to be criticized by one whom the people detested.

Christ might have glorified Himself there and then. He might have shown a power that would have made His judges quail. He knew that He was appointed to His office by God. But a body of flesh had been prepared for Him. He concealed His divinity by a garb of humanity. Being found in fashion as a man, He humbled Himself, that He might be qualified to represent man in the heavenly courts. He took not on Him the nature even of angels. The highest of all angels, He girded Himself with a towel, and washed the feet of His disciples. He mourned and wept over the perversity and transgression of men. He did not rend His robe, but His soul was rent. His garment of human flesh was rent as He hung on the cross, the Sin-bearer of the human race. By His suffering and death, a new and living way was opened. By this He was to enter upon His priestly office forever. There was no longer a wall of partition between Jew and Gentile. As the high priest for the whole world, He entered the holy place.[52]

What glorious truth! A way was opened for all, Jew and Gentile alike, to approach the Father. The mystery "that the Gentiles should be fellowheirs, and of the same body, and partakers of his promise in Christ by the gospel" (Eph. 3:6) was revealed. His "house shall be called an house of prayer for all people," for "the sons of the stranger, that join themselves to the LORD" will He bring to His "holy mountain" (Isa. 56:7, 3, 6). Christ has "broken down the middle wall of partition between us; Having abolished in his flesh the enmity ... that he might reconcile both unto God in one body by the cross" (Eph. 2:14–16). That which "was against us, which was contrary to us," He "took it out of the way, nailing it to his cross" (Col. 2:15).

Such are the truths revealed by that "new and living way" (Heb. 10:20), which the falsities promoted in *Within the Veil* cover by bringing "in dirt and shavings and sand and all manner of rubbish."[53]

---

52   Manuscript Releases, vol. 12, pp. 399, 400.
53   Ellen G. White, Early Writings (Washington, D.C.: Review and Herald Publishing Association, 1882), p. 83.

Notice the plain words of Christ on this point:

"Verily, verily, I say unto you, He that heareth my word, and believeth on him that sent me, hath everlasting life, and shall not come into condemnation; but is passed from death unto life." John 5:24

The word used for "condemnation" is "krisis" which Strongs states as follows:

Greek: κρίσις

Transliteration: krisis

Pronunciation: kree'-sis

Definition: (Subjectively or objectively for or against); by extension a tribunal; by implication justice (specifically divine law): - accusation condemnation damnation judgment.

KJV Usage: judgment (41x), damnation (3x), accusation (2x), condemnation (2x).

Occurrences in Bible: 48

Occurrences in verses: 47

So Jesus states that those who believe on him do not come into judgment; that is, a tribunal with the basis of the divine law. Yet this is exactly what SDA's teach: that Christians who place their faith in Christ, who become new creatures in Christ, who have their consciences purged from dead works to serve the living God, who have been washed and regenerated and renewed by the Holy Ghost, who have been reconciled to God by the death of His Son, who have been adopted into God's family and translated into the kingdom of his dear son, who have been sanctified and who have received the atonement (all phrases used by the New Testament authors), suddenly in 1844 by a fluke of prophecy now have all of their sins brought to remembrance and are closely investigated to see whether they are saved. Yet all of this in the face of God's word which declares that "the Lord knoweth them that are His". 2 Timothy 2:19.

To further prove this point, and that the sins of believers are blotted out once they are confessed and forsaken, and not in 1844; and that it is impossible that the righteous dead would come up in judgment in 1844 when their cases would supposedly come up before God, thus not allowing for their sins to be blotted out until that time, I submit the following evidence:

Moses was resurrected and taken to heaven prior to 1844, before which time his sins supposedly would have been brought up in judgment and blotted out.

As was Enoch translated to heaven prior to his case being decided in 1844.

As was Elijah.

As was the great multitude of witnesses who were resurrected after Christ's resurrection.

And all of this prior to 1844 when their books were supposed to be opened and their cases eternally decided in an investigative judgment for the righteous. So either God judged them worthy of eternal life and blotted out their sins prior to taking them all to heaven, and the theory of an investigative judgment commencing in 1844 is incorrect; or SDA theology is correct and the SOP (writings of Ellen White) is correct at the expense of God contradicting himself and making the Bible a mockery.

I haven't even mentioned the souls under the altar (Rev. 6:9–11) who were judged righteous and given white robes under the fifth seal which was also prior to the dark day, etc, under the sixth seal and prior to 1844. Nor did I mention Ellen White *stating that she saw Fitch and Stockman in heaven in vision, along with Abraham, Isaac, Jacob, and others...does this mean that their cases had been decided by December of 1844 only two months after the great day of atonement had commenced? The whole theology is unsound.[54]*

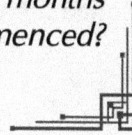

The basis of this argumentative point is a faulty understanding of the surrounding context of John 5:24. When a good student of Scripture considers this verse as one should, the context determines that the judgment passed by the righteous is the execution phase allotted to the wicked (see verses 21–30). Another way of reading the verse is, "He that hears my word, and believes on him that sent me, has everlasting life, and shall not come into the condemnation of the judgment." That understanding is consistent with the rest of the biblical testimony concerning a judgment for both the wicked, with their evil deeds, and the righteous, with their goods deeds (see Eccles. 3:16, 17; 12:13, 14; Rom. 14:10–12; 2 Cor. 5:10; Rev. 22:12). Those accounted worthy (see Luke 20:35; 21:36) by individual inspection (see Eccles. 7:27) "shall not come into condemnation" (John 5:24) because "there is therefore now no condemnation to them which are in Christ Jesus" (Rom. 8:1).

Christ dwells in the heart of the believer by faith (Eph. 3:17), and wherever Christ is, there is the resurrection and the fountain of life. "He that believeth on the Son, hath everlasting life." Jn. 3:33. "Verily, verily, I say unto you, He that heareth My word, and believeth on Him that sent Me, hath everlasting life, and shall not come into condemnation; but is passed from death until

---

54   Within the Veil, pp. 6, 7.

life." Jn. 5:25. Such an one [sic] has already entered the portal to eternal life and happiness, and no power can draw him back, for there is nothing that is able to separate the soul from Him. (Rom. 8:38, 39).[55]

As mentioned above, the points were taught clearly by Christ when He said:

> For God so loved the world, that he gave his only begotten Son, that whosoever believeth in him should not perish, but have everlasting life. For God sent not his Son into the world to condemn the world; but that the world through him might be saved. He that believeth on him is not condemned: but he that believeth not is condemned already, because he hath not believed in the name of the only begotten Son of God. And this is the condemnation, that light is come into the world, and men loved darkness rather than light, because their deeds were evil. (John 3:16–19)

One saying of the Savior must not be leveraged to disparage another, and to be frank, the cherry-picking used throughout *Within the Veil* does just that. The truth of the judgment has been ensured by Jesus' resurrection (see Acts 17:30, 31) and was part of the original Christian faith (see verses 24, 25). The Bible teaches that there are two phases to this judgment: one, to acquit the saints and vindicate the character of God (see Dan. 7:9, 10, 13, 14, 21, 22), and the other, to execute upon the wicked the judgment written and obliterate sin (see Rev. 20:4, 5, 11–15; cf. Ps. 149:5–9; 1 Cor. 6:1–3). Many dispute the introduction of judgment on behalf of the saints in Daniel 7, believing it is wrongly applied and, as such, should instead be upon the "little horn" (verse 8). However, Daniel clarifies who the recipients of the judgment are by saying, "judgment was given to the saints of the most High" (verse 22).

We have already addressed Daniel 7:22 in the sixth contention, but currently under examination, this eighth contention necessitates its review. The prophet beholds the papacy "mak[ing] war with the saints," and it "prevailed against them" for 1,260 years (verses 21, 25), from AD 538 to 1798, "until the Ancient of days came, and judgment was given to the saints of the most High" (verse 22), October 22, 1844. The phrase

---

55 Ellet J. Waggoner, "A Gloomy Doctrine," *The Present Truth*, October 25 1894, p. 380.

"judgment was given to the saints" in the Authorized Version is translated as "judgment was made in favor of the saints" (NKJV), "pronounced judgment in favor of the holy people" (NIV), "judgment was rendered in favor of the holy ones" (NET), "judgment was given for the saints" (ESV, RSV), and "judgment was passed in favor of the saints" (NASB). In each translation, the subjects of the judgment are the righteous, not the wicked; the judgment of the wicked cannot begin until the coming of the Lord (see Jude 1:14, 15). The judgment is taken up again in Daniel 8 under the symbol of cleansing the sanctuary (verse 14) and, as we have previously learned, represents the antitypical day of atonement.

Another point with which we take issue is Richards' allegation against the Seventh-day Adventist view of forgiveness, which he used to force his point. He stated that Seventh-day Adventists teach "that Christians who place their faith in Christ, who become new creatures in Christ, who have their consciences purged from dead works to serve the living God ... suddenly in 1844 by a fluke of prophecy now have all of their sins brought to remembrance and are closely investigated to see whether they are saved."[56] That is not the teaching of Seventh-day Adventism at all, and Richards, being a former Seventh-day Adventist himself, knows that well.

Asserting that our sins are "brought to remembrance" during the judgment assumes that, at some point, they were forgotten. Seventh-day Adventists believe the forgiveness of sin and the blotting out of sin are separate things, while Richards believes "the sins of believers are blotted out once they are confessed and forsaken."[57] However, such a belief flies in the face of Bible truth. The apostle Peter, under the direct influence of the Holy Spirit (see Acts 2:1–4), stated that the blotting out of sins takes place "when the times of refreshing shall come from the presence of the Lord"

> *Asserting that our sins are "brought to remembrance" during the judgment assumes that, at some point, they were forgotten. Seventh-day Adventists believe the forgiveness of sin and the blotting out of sin are separate things, while Richards believes "the sins of believers are blotted out once they are confessed and forsaken." However, such a belief flies in the face of Bible truth.*

56   Within the Veil, p. 6.
57   *Ibid.*

(3:19), not when they are confessed and forsaken.

Mr. Wesley, in his "Notes on the New Testament," gives a different translation, which may be more accurate:

"Repent ye therefore, and be converted, that your sins may be blotted out, that the times of refreshing may come from the presence of the Lord, and he may send to you Jesus Christ, who was before appointed."

Albert Barnes, in his "Notes on the Acts," speaking of these two translations, says, "The grammatical construction will admit of either." One of these represents the blotting out to be when the times of refreshing arrive; the other makes it the cause of that refreshing. But neither of them gives the idea that this blotting out takes place when the sinner turns to God. Both of them throw it into the future. Each of them represents it as preceding the second coming of the Lord. But this is especially true of the latter translation, which follows the original in using a conditional verb respecting Christ's advent; not as though that were a doubtful event, but rather as if his coming to the personal salvation of the ones addressed depended upon their having part in the refreshing, and as if that refreshing was to come in consequence of the blotting out of sins.

The sins of the righteous are blotted out before the coming of Christ. They cannot be called to give account of their sins after they have been blotted out; whence it follows that whatever account the righteous render to God for their sins must be before the advent of the Saviour, and not at, or after, that event.

3. The sins of men are written in the books of God's remembrance. The blotting out of the sins of the righteous does therefore involve the examination of these books for this very purpose. That the sins of men are thus written, is plainly revealed in the Scriptures.

"For though thou wash thee with niter, and take thee much soap, yet *thine iniquity is marked before me*, saith the Lord God." Jeremiah 2:22. And thus the Lord speaks of the guilt of Israel: "Is not this *laid up in store with me*, and sealed up among my treasures?" Deuteronomy 32:34. And Paul speaks in the same manner: "But after thy hardness and impenitent heart *treasureth up* unto thyself wrath against the day of wrath and revelation of the righteous judgment of God; who will render to every man according to his deeds." Romans 2:5, 6. These statements of wrath being treasured up can have reference only to the fact that God takes notice of men's sins, and that every sin is marked before him. To this fact all the texts which speak of the blotting out of sins must have reference. Thus David prays that God would *blot out* his transgressions. Psalm 51:1, 9. And Nehemiah, and David, and Jeremiah, pray respecting certain persons, that their sin may *not be blotted out*. Nehemiah 4:5; Psalm 109:14; Jeremiah 18:23. And Isaiah, in prophetic language, speaks of this blotting out as if it were a *past* event, just as in the next verse he speaks of the new creation, and the final redemption. Isaiah 44:22, 23. And in the previous chapter he speaks in a similar manner of this blotting out as necessary in order that the sins of the people of God may be no more remembered. Isaiah 43:25. These texts plainly imply that the sins of men are upon record, and that there is a time when these are blotted out of the record of the righteous.[58]

That Bible doctrine is emphasized further by the parable of the unforgiving servant (see Matt. 18:23–35). Although the king forgave his debt (see verse 27), its record was still on the books and placed upon his account afresh by his act of unforgiveness (see verses 28–34). Jesus enforces this truth by closing with the words, "So likewise shall my heavenly Father do also unto you" (verse 35) to explain the parable's meaning. The parable plainly illustrates the conditional nature of forgiveness and shows how past forgiveness can be nullified by present or future sin. That is our Savior's view of forgiveness under the gospel (justification by faith) while we are waiting for the decision of the judgment.

Some argue that Paul teaches that we have already received the atonement (see Rom. 5:11). However, the Greek word *katallage*, translated as "atonement" in the verse, should be rendered "reconciliation," like in the margin and notes for the Authorized Version. Repentance and the intercession of our great High Priest above effect reconciliation between us and God. However, the atonement (i.e., the blotting out or removing) of sins so they can be remembered no more against us is the last act of priestly service performed

---

58   Andrews, *The Judgment: Its Events and Their Order* (Oakland, CA: Pacific Press Publishing Company, 1890), pp. 12, 13.

by the Lord for us (see Lev. 16:20–22). Forgiving sin and blotting out sin is not the same. Forgiveness is conditional. We must comply with the requirements upon which it is hung until the end of our probation. If we fail, we will stand before God unforgiven, and no atonement can be made for us. The same may be said of every case where the word "atonement" is applied in the present tense (as it frequently is in Leviticus) before the great Day of Atonement; they were all conditional. Everything depended on acceptance when the general atonement was made at the close of the yearly service.

The prophet Ezekiel states this truth: "When a righteous man turneth away from his righteousness, and committeth iniquity, and dieth in them; for his iniquity that he hath done shall he die"; "all his righteousnesses shall not be remembered" (18:26; 33:13). The Lord will treat this person like he or she had never been righteous. The righteousness of the saints is by faith; therefore, if one turns and commits iniquity, that person shall be treated as if he or she never had faith; the forgiveness, conditionally extended, is withdrawn.

> How, then, if the atonement is yet future, do we receive of its benefits? How are we justified? In reply, we would ask the questioner, How, if the atonement was made on the cross, did those who lived before that time secure its benefits? And just as the people of God who lived and died before Christ could receive the benefits of the atonement if it was made on the cross, just so both they and we can receive its benefits, if it is deferred to be the closing work of this dispensation. It is by faith. The patriarchs were justified by faith, and so died. So with the righteous ever since that day. All their life-work, their acts of faith, stand faithfully written out in the heavenly books of record. The time comes for the investigative Judgment, for the last division of Christ's work as priest, for the sanctuary to be cleansed, for sins to be blotted out, for the atonement to be made. The books are opened. Every case is examined. Then the sins of those whose record shows their last acts to have been acts of repentance, faith, and obedience, are atoned for, or blotted out.[59]

The opposing view emphasizes that atonement was completed on the cross, and sin once confessed and forsaken is blotted out, but that is profuse

---

59   Smith, *The Sanctuary and the Twenty-Three Hundred Days of Daniel 8:14* (Battle Creek, MI: Seventh-day Adventist Publishing Association, 1877), p. 281.

with the errors of the "once saved, always saved" theology. The Scriptures teach that one can fall away; therefore, one's salvation is conditional (see Heb. 6:4–8; 3:12–19; 10:26–31; cf. Ex. 32:32, 33; Jude 1:5; Rev. 3:5) and, as shown, is determined by the judgment, where God will "render to every man according to his deeds"—righteous and wicked (Rom. 2:6). Furthermore, the judgment passes upon "the quick [living] and the dead" (1 Peter 4:5, 6), which brings to light that those saints who were translated, like Enoch and Elijah, or resurrected, like Moses and the multitude of witnesses, have to be deemed righteous according to the law (see Eccles. 12:13, 14; Isa. 26:1, 2; Rev. 2:7; 4:4; 3:5; 22:14).

These saints, taken to glory before the judgment—some, even before the cross—were credited with salvation. Like Jesus, who was awarded His kingdom based upon Him completing His work though waiting in expectancy for it (see Dan. 7:13, 14; Heb. 10:12, 13), these righteous ones were given the saints' reward based upon Him completing that ministry. Like all of God's children, they "were sealed with that holy Spirit of promise, which is the earnest of our inheritance" (Eph. 1:13, 14; cf. Rom. 8:15–17, 22–25; 2 Cor. 1:21, 22; 5:5–10). The Greek word translated "earnest" is *arrhabon*, meaning "a pledge or down payment that the total amount will subsequently be paid." The all-knowing God can give the reward before all the conditions are met because "the Lord knoweth them that are his" (2 Tim. 2:19).

The language of this prophecy states in the original: "And he said unto me, Unto two thousand and three hundred days; then shall the sanctuary be justified or vindicated or set right". The Hebrew word for "cleansed" is "tsadaq" which means:

Hebrew: קדצ

Transliteration: tsâdaq

Pronunciation: tsaw-dak'

Definition: A primitive root; to be (causatively make) right (in a moral or forensic sense): - {cleanse} clear {self} ({be} do) just ({-ice} {-ify} -ify {self}) ({be} turn to) righteous (-ness).

KJV Usage: justify (23x), righteous (10x), just (3x), justice (2x), cleansed (1x), clear ourselves (1x), righteousness (1x).

Occurrences in Bible: 41

Occurrences in verses: 40

This is a different word than the word used in Leviticus 16 for the day of atonement cleansing.

In other words, after 2300 days God's sanctuary would be set right and vindicated from the activity of the ... power which trampled it under foot and cast the truth to ground "and practiced and prospered". In fact, in every reference of a judgment sitting and books being opened, it is referring to judgment on the papal power and on the wicked in general, and to the vindication of the righteous. See Daniel 7:8-27; 8:14-25; Revelation 20:11-15. And it is the same with the 3 angels' messages of Revelation 14. In context, the judgment hour message of the first angel is connected with a declaration of judgment on Babylon and the consequences of worshipping the beast and his image delineated in the second and third messages.

Our current understanding of the 2300 day prophecy, as far as starting and ending dates is concerned, hasn't changed at this point. We still believe in the day/year principle and the starting date of 457BC [sic] according to Daniel 9 which brings the end date to 1844. But I believe the prophecy is misunderstood based on the text. The phrase "then shall the sanctuary be cleansed" we have historically applied to the day of atonement when this is not possible given the context or language of the chapter. The word used for "cleansed" is not the same word used in Leviticus 16. The original says "then shall the sanctuary be justified or set right". The word for cleansed in Daniel 8:14 is the same word used in 2 Chronicles 29:15-18 when the temple was cleansed and set right from being defiled with pagan idolatry. And this what [sic] Daniel 8 is teaching as well. The question from the angel to Christ was "how long shall paganism and papalism trample the sanctuary and host?" And the answer is given "unto 2300 days, then shall the sanctuary be set right or justified or cleansed from pagan idolatry". So in 1844 the filth and errors of Rome would finally be purged from God's church on earth, which work began with the Protestant reformation [sic] with Luther and the doctrine of justification by faith, continued through that time with the restoration of other truths such as baptism by immersion for believers, the true meaning of the Lords supper, the Sabbath, and completed with the truth of soul sleep in death, hellfire and the destruction of the wicked, and the understanding of Christ's high priestly ministry in the heavenly sanctuary.[60]

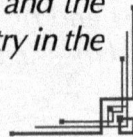

---

60   Within the Veil, pp. 7, 8.

A war of words began with the eighth contention by delving into the original language to understand the text. We have contributed by using Hebrew and Greek or quoting from authors who used the same, as well as different versions of the Bible. However, we want the reader to understand that while a valuable resource, knowledge of Hebrew and Greek is unnecessary when studying the Scriptures. The Bible student can rely upon the English language, comparing Bible text with Bible text, following the principles outlined in Isaiah 28:10 and of Bible interpretation given to William Miller.[61] That does not mean, however, that the original language lacks value; instead, it points to the fact that God "will guard the translation of his own word, and throw a barrier around it, and prevent those who sincerely trust in God, and put implicit confidence in his word, from erring far from the truth, though they may not understand Hebrew or Greek."[62] Inspiration has stated, "Those who are engaged in proclaiming the third angel's message are searching the Scriptures upon the same plan that Father Miller adopted."[63]

In this ninth objection, the focus is an issue with the word "cleansed" in Daniel 8:14. The translators of the KJV, as well as those of the NKJV, DRA, ERV, ASV, WEB, GNV, BBE, etc., saw fit to render the Hebrew word *tsadaq* as the English word "cleansed" or "made clean" in the text, and based upon the definition offered by Richards in *Within the Veil*, they are not wrong. Looking at the meaning supplied in his ninth point, we see that *tsadaq*'s definition is "to be (causatively make) right (in a moral or forensic sense)." In other words, something would make it morally or legally right. The words and/or phrases supplied to describe how that would take place are "to justify," "to be (become) righteous," and "to cleanse." *Young's Analytical Concordance to the Bible* defines *tsadaq* as "to become, be counted righteous." The *Brown-Driver-Briggs Hebrew and English Lexicon* (Unabridged) renders the phrase "then shall the sanctuary be cleansed [*tsadaq*]" as "the holy place shall be put right, in a right condition."

---

61   See Apollos Hale, The Second Advent Manual (Boston: Joshua V. Himes, 1843), pp. 102–106.
62   *Ibid.*, p. 105.
63   Ellen G. White, "Notes of Travel," The Review and Herald, November 25, 1884.

> *Candid Bible students should ask themselves what it might be that would make the sanctuary unjust, unrighteous, or unclean in a moral or legal sense in the first place. The only answers one can give while being honest with the totality of Scripture is iniquity, transgression, and sin ...*

Candid Bible students should ask themselves what it might be that would make the sanctuary unjust, unrighteous, or unclean in a moral or legal sense in the first place. The only answers one can give while being honest with the totality of Scripture is iniquity, transgression, and sin; that is especially true when one considers the word "cleanse," as offered by the original language. Transgressing the law (see Gen. 3:6, 7; cf. 1 John 3:4) made the sacrificial system (see Gen. 3:21; 4:3–5) and the sanctuary services (see Exod. 24:1–31:18) necessary object lessons depicting the plan of salvation. As the sanctuary plan was laid out before Moses, and through him to the people, the Lord made it abundantly clear that the uncleanness of sin needed removal by the ministration of the high priest on what became known as the Day of Atonement (see Lev. 16:1–34; 23:27–32; 25:9).

Understand that desecration of the earthly sanctuary happened in other ways also (see Ezek. 8:5–18, 9:5–7; 2 Chron. 33:1–9; Jer. 23:11, 32:34), but the sanctuary highlighted in Daniel 8:14 is not the earthly sanctuary; instead, it is the heavenly. In AD 1844, the ending year for the 2,300-day prophecy, there was no earthly sanctuary to defile. There is also no corresponding historical event concerning "God's church on earth"[64] in 1844 that would fulfill Richards' understanding of the cleansing or setting right of the sanctuary.

First of all, that time prophecy relates to the sanctuary, not to the people or "host" (verse 13). Second, as was already stated, there was no earthly sanctuary for the papacy to defile. Pagan Rome destroyed that temple in AD 70 to fulfill Christ's prophecy (see Matt. 24:1–3, 15–18; Mark 13:1–4, 14–16; Luke 21:5–7, 20–22; cf. Dan. 9:26). Third, if in "1844 the filth and errors of Rome would finally be purged from God's church on earth, which work began with the Protestant reformation [sic] with Luther and the doctrine of justification by faith,"[65] as taught in *Within the Veil*, the time prophecy would not find its termination in 1844.

---

64   Within the Veil, p. 8.
65   *Ibid.*

The angel's question, "How long shall be the vision concerning the daily [paganism], and the transgression of desolation [papalism], to give both the sanctuary and the host to be trodden under foot?" (Dan. 8:13) places the beginning of the prophecy before the rise of the papacy, as far back as the Medo-Persian empire. To teach that the prophecy's fulfillment "began with the Protestant reformation [sic] with Luther and the doctrine of justification by faith"[66] places its beginning in 1517!

Finally, teaching that the purging of errors and "restoration of" truth would culminate with the "understanding of Christ's high priestly ministry in the heavenly sanctuary"[67] in 1844 would only serve to give validity to the Seventh-day Adventist understanding of Christ's high priestly work—a very curious position to take in a paper that was written to undermine Seventh-day Adventism's foundation and central pillar.[68]

With all the aforementioned in place, let us turn to the Bible and see if justifying or setting something right is congruent with cleansing. If so, the argument in *Within the Veil* is baseless.

Bildad the Shuhite questioned how a man can "be justified with God?" then followed with the equivalent, "how can he be clean that is born of a woman?" (Job 25:4). In this verse, we see that being justified and being made clean are interchangeable. David, in his famous psalm, supplicates the throne of God, asking Him to "wash" him thoroughly from his "iniquity" and "cleanse" him from his sin (Ps. 51:2), and he connects that cleansing with the blotting out of sin and God's fair judgment (see verse 1, 4), the very nature of the work our heavenly High Priest is even now in the process of accomplishing. The apostle Paul also connects washing with being justified (see 1 Cor. 6:9–11; Titus 3:5–7).

In light of the English language, the Bible clarifies that the cleansing of the sanctuary above, as stated in Daniel 8:14, aligns with the Hebraic understanding of its being justified morally or legally. The ceremonial cleansing of the sanctuary on the Day of Atonement, on the tenth day of the seventh month, in type, served as a means of cleansing the people from their moral and legal transgression of the law (see Lev. 16:29–33). The final atoning work of Christ above in the heavenly sanctuary, which commenced on October 22, 1844, is the antitypical fulfillment of the annual cleansing of the earthly sanctuary (see verse 29; 23:27).

---

66   *Ibid.*
67   *Ibid.*
68   See Ellen G. White, *The Spirit of Prophecy*, vol. 4 (Battle Creek, MI: Seventh-day Adventist Publishing Association, 1884), p. 258.

In order to preserve an [sic] historic identity, the SDA church has sought to portray the doctrine of the investigative judgment as unique among themselves and as standing as repairers of the breach in pointing the world to the broken law of God that the papacy sought to obscure and to change. Therefore, 1844 has stood as a pivotal date where God is now judging men based on his law now revealed in the most holy place to the world, of which the Sabbath truth is the testing point. Yet history is clear that there have always been witnesses for truth throughout the ages who have kept the commandments of God and the faith of Jesus, including the Sabbath. Also, both before and after 1844, such groups as the seventh-day Baptists held the Sabbath truth out to the world and presented the 10 commandments as binding, all without the necessity of showing the date of 1844 as being a commencement date to make the Sabbath of force since that time. How can SDA's claim that they are the sole people to stand as repairers of the breach since 1844 if others were already in existence prior to this time who did the same, and even were the ones to share this truth with them?[69]

Yes, "history is clear that there have always been witnesses for truth throughout the ages who have kept the commandments of God and the faith of Jesus, including the Sabbath."[70] That statement solicits no retort from us, since we agree.

---

69   Within the Veil, pp. 8, 9.
70   Ibid., p. 8.

Its purpose, however, is to place the Seventh-day Adventist faith in question, both in nature and purpose, and so we will address that point.

Richards, a defender of the Seventh-day Adventist faith for fifteen years, now wandered away, calls into question its identity. He asks, "How can SDA's claim that they are the sole people to stand as repairers of the breach since 1844 if others were already in existence prior to this time who did the same, and even were the ones to share this truth with them?"[71] In other words, Seventh-day Adventists are the new kids on the block and got the Sabbath from the Seventh Day Baptists, whose movement originated in the mid-17th century. Therefore, Seventh-day Adventists, whose denomination grew out of the Millerite movement during the mid-19th century, are not unique—a borderline "the older church is the better church" argument.

While the Seventh Day Baptist movement originated earlier than the Seventh-day Adventist movement did, Seventh-day Adventists can claim a purer faith. The Seventh Day Baptists' understanding of the Godhead, false view of the state of the dead and eternal hellfire, and false interpretation of Bible prophecy are positions of faith that are not consistent with Scripture. While they hold the Sabbath in common, Seventh Day Baptists tend to hold a vaguer position concerning it, while Seventh-day Adventists consider it as the sign or seal of God (see Exod. 31:13, 16, 17; Ezek. 20:12, 20) and soon to be the great test for humanity (see Rev. 13:11–17; 14:9–11).

———————————

71   *Ibid.*, pp. 8, 9.

Seventh-day Adventists find the origin of their movement in Bible prophecy (see Rev. 10, 12–14) as the capstone of the Protestant Reformation. The corruption of the Roman Church and its persecution against dissenters (see 12:13) forced the Christian church into seclusion for 1,260 years (see verses 6, 14), from AD 538 to 1798. The church, however, was not to remain in obscurity forever. As surely as it went into the "wilderness," it would come out of it. Christ's church, "the pillar and ground of the truth" (1 Tim. 3:15), had a mission that was to last even until the end of the world (see Matt. 28:19, 20). According to prophecy, the earth (see Rev. 12:15, 16), a symbol of the New World—the United States of America—helped the hiding church. Therefore, we should see this prophetic church emerge in the United States after 1798 in fulfillment of the Scriptures. The Seventh Day Baptist movement cannot fulfill this prophecy because its birth was in England in the 1600s, and even when appearing in America (specifically, Newport, Rhode Island—calling themselves Sabbatarian Baptists), it was the mid-1600s. Seventh-day Adventism arose in the mid-1800s in America.

Prophecy also distinguishes other marks of this prophetic church by showing it keeps "the commandments of God" and has "the testimony of Jesus Christ" (Rev. 12:17), which is "the spirit of prophecy" (19:10). Though the Seventh Day Baptist faith keeps all ten of the commandments, they flunk the biblical test of having "the testimony of Jesus Christ." In the angel's own words, he was John's "fellowservant" and of his "brethren that have the testimony of Jesus" (verse 10), which he later identified as "the prophets" (22:9). Since the prophets are the ones who have it, the "testimony of Jesus" or the "spirit of prophecy" is the spiritual gift of prophecy (see 1 Cor. 12; Eph. 4:8–16). The existence of this gift, along with the keeping of all the commandments of God, are two biblical identifying marks of Christ's church in the last days. The Seventh Day Baptists do not measure up, taking the stance that there are no modern-day prophets since the Bible canon closed. However, the spiritual gifts are promised to the church until the end (see 1 Cor. 13:9, 10; cf. Mark 16:15–18; Matt. 28:20), and the gift of prophecy is the gift of preference, primarily benefiting the church (see 1 Cor. 14:1, 22). On the other hand, the Seventh-day Adventist Church keeps the ten commandments and has a prophet fulfilling the prophecy.

Pointing out that the Seventh Day Baptist faith fails to fulfill the Scriptures' last-day church does not mean Seventh Day Baptists were not influential in promoting truth; instead, it shows they are not the church to which the Lord points in Bible prophecy. Nevertheless, He powerfully used them:

Rachel Oakes Preston (1809–1868) a Seventh Day Baptist from Verona, New York, brought Seventh Day teaching to a small Millerite group that became the SDAs in Washington, New Hampshire. Through her influence, Frederick Wheeler became the first SDA preacher. One family, the Cottrells, looked favorably upon William Miller's Second Advent message but did not join the movement prior to 1844 because it did not acknowledge the seventh-day Sabbath. After a group of Adventists accepted the Sabbath, the Cottrells joined them. Later on, in the 1860s and '70s, the leadership of the two organizations associated with each other. They recognized their common interest in promoting Sabbath observance. Adventist pioneer James Springer White went so far as to advise Adventist preachers not to conduct evangelistic campaigns in the small towns with a Seventh Day Baptist presence.[72]

Most of the Lord's children are not a part of the last-day church (see John 10:16), yet He gives a final message of mercy to call them to come in (see Rev. 14:6–12). The Seventh Day Baptists dismiss this final warning as an "emphasis on human effort" and call it "remnant theology."[73] Seventh-day Adventists consider the three angels' messages of Revelation 14 as their message, work, and calling.

Seventh Day Baptists have no prophetic claim to being the movement the Lord will use to close this earth's history. However, their many faithful members will no doubt be a part of that final work when the call goes forth to "Come out of her, my people" (Rev. 18:4). We pray that brother Richards—although not explicitly claiming to be a Seventh Day Baptist but rather a Baptist[74]—will also participate in that glorious closing work and that his "sins may be blotted out, when the times of refreshing shall come from the presence of the Lord" (Acts 3:19).

---

72   "Seventh Day Baptists," Wikipedia, last modified November 13, 2023, https://en.wikipedia.org/wiki/Seventh_Day_Baptists.

73   "Did You Say Seventh Day Baptist? A Comparison of Seventh Day Baptists and Seventh-Day Adventists," Association of Seventh Day Baptists Australia, https://www.isdba.org/_files/ugd/bcd-c7f_3a6f85045d644bfc968eea3d1d13bc37.pdf.

74   See "ABOUT US," Independent Seventh Day Bible Baptist Association, https://www.isdba.org/about-us.

BIBLIOGRAPHY

"A Comparison of Seventh Day Baptists and Seventh-day Adventists," Independent Seventh Day Baptist Association. https://www.isdba.org/sdb-vs-sda (accessed January 2, 2020).

"ABOUT US." Independent Seventh Day Bible Baptist Association. https://www.isdba.org/about-us.

Andrews, John N. *The Judgment: Its Events and Their Order*. Oakland, CA: Pacific Press Publishing Company, 1890.

_____. *The Sanctuary and Twenty-Three Hundred Days*. Battle Creek, MI: Steam Press of the Seventh-day Adventist Publishing Association, 1872.

Bates, Joseph. *[Bates' Pamphlet #3] An Explanation of the Typical and Anti-Typical Sanctuary by the Scriptures*. Press of Benjamin Lindsey, 1850.

Bliss, Sylvester. *Memoirs of William Miller*. Boston: Joshua V. Himes, 1853.

Crosier, Owen R. L. *The Sanctuary*. Auburn, NY: Advent Review, 1850.

"Did You Say Seventh Day Baptist? A Comparison of Seventh Day Baptists and Seventh-Day Adventists." Association of Seventh Day Baptists Australia. https://www.isdba.org/_files/ugd/bcdc7f_3a6f85045d644bf-c968eea3d1d13bc37.pdf.

Froom, LeRoy Edwin. *The Prophetic Faith of Our Fathers*. Vol. 4 Washington, D.C.: Review and Herald Publishing Association, 1954.

Hale, Apollos. *The Second Advent Manual*. Boston: Joshua V. Himes, 1843.

Hardinge, Leslie. *With Jesus in His Sanctuary*. 1st ed. Harrisburg, PA: American Cassette Ministries, Book Division, 1991.

Haskell, Stephen N. *The Cross and Its Shadow*. South Lancaster, MA: The Bible Training School, 1914.

Jones, Alonzo T. *The Consecrated Way to Christian Perfection.* Mountain View, CA: Pacific Press Publishing Company, 1905.

Richards, J. Isaac. *Within the Veil.* Gakona, AK: Independent Seventh Day Bible Baptist Association, 2019. https://www.isdba.org/_files/ugd/bcd-c7f_8eafd31002ea4e7ab103ae6393cf1ba7.pdf.

Smith, Uriah. *The Biblical Institute.* Oakland, CA: Pacific Seventh-day Adventist Publishing House, 1878.

_____. *The Sanctuary and the Twenty-Three Hundred Days of Daniel 8:14.* Battle Creek, MI: Seventh-day Adventist Publishing Association, 1877.

Waggoner, Ellet J. "A Gloomy Doctrine." *The Present Truth,* October 25, 1894.

White, Ellen G. *The Acts of the Apostles.* Mountain View, CA: Pacific Press Publishing Association, 1911.

_____. *Christ's Object Lessons.* Review and Herald Publishing Association, 1900.

_____. *The Desire of Ages.* Mountain View, CA: Pacific Press Publishing Association, 1898.

_____. *Early Writings.* Washington, D.C.: Review and Herald Publishing Association, 1882.

_____. *God's Amazing Grace.* Washington, D.C.: Review and Herald Publishing Association, 1973.

_____. *The Great Controversy.* Mountain View, CA: Pacific Press Publishing Association, 1911.

_____. *Letters and Manuscripts.* Vol. 22. Lt 230. Ellen G. White Estate, 1907.

_____. *Manuscript Releases.* Vol. 12. Silver Spring, MD: Ellen G. White Estate, 1990.

_____. "Our Sacrifice." *The Signs of the Times,* December 8, 1898.

_____. "Power for Service." *The Signs of the Times,* August 19, 1903.

_____. "The Price of Our Redemption." *The Youth's Instructor,* June 21, 1900.

_____. *Selected Messages*. Book. 1. Washington, D.C.: Review and Herald Publishing Association, 1958.

_____. *The SDA Bible Commentary*. Vol. 7. Washington, D.C.: Review and Herald Publishing Association, 1957.

_____. *The SDA Bible Commentary*. Vol. 7A. Washington, D.C.: Review and Herald Publishing Association, 1970.

_____. *The Spirit of Prophecy*. Vol. 4. Battle Creek, MI: Seventh-day Adventist Publishing Association, 1884.

_____. "What Was Secured by the Death of Christ." *The Signs of the Times*, December 30, 1889.

White, James S. *Bible Adventism*. Battle Creek, MI: Seventh-day Adventist Publishing Association, n.d.

Wikipedia. "Seventh Day Baptists." Last modified November 13, 2023. https://en.wikipedia.org/wiki/Seventh_Day_Baptists

The Geneva Bible. Powder Springs, GA: Tolle Lege Press, 1599.

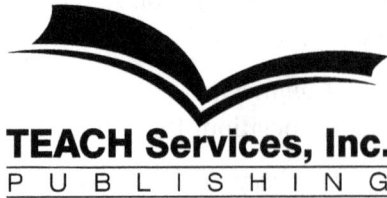

www.ingramcontent.com/pod-product-compliance
Lightning Source LLC
Chambersburg PA
CBHW060554100426
42742CB00013B/2554